Subtraction of Larger

Turn to each section to find a more detailed skills list.

Table of Contents

What Does This Book Include?

- More than 80 student practice pages that build basic math skills
- A detailed skills list for each section of the book
- Send-home letters informing parents of the skills being targeted and ways to practice these skills
- Student checkups
- A reproducible student progress chart
- Reproducible grids to use with students who need help aligning numbers properly when writing vertical subtraction problems
- Awards to celebrate student progress
- Answer keys for easy checking
- Perforated pages for easy removal and filing if desired

What Are the Benefits of This Book?

- Is organized for quick and easy use
- Enhances and supports your existing math program
- Offers two to five reproducible practice pages for each subtraction skill
- Provides reinforcement for different ability levels
- Includes communication pages that encourage parent participation in the child's learning of math
- Contains checkups that assess students' subtraction knowledge
- Offers a reproducible chart for documenting student progress
- Aligns with national math standards

Manufactured in the United States
10 9 8 7 6 5 4 3 2 1

How to Use This Book
Steps to Success

Choose Skills to Target

Scan the detailed table of contents at the beginning of each section to find just the right skills to target your students' needs.

Select Fun Practice Pages

From a variety of fun formats, choose the pages that best match your students' current ability levels.

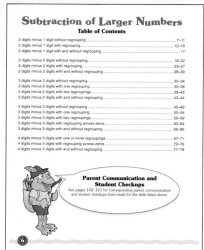

Parent Communication and Student Checkups
See pages 102–121 for corresponding parent communication and student checkups (mini tests) for the skills listed above.

6

Fun Formats

Date Skill Completed

Computer Solutions

Stargazers

Pond Pals

Movie Munchies

Targeted Skill

Letter to Parents Informing Them of Skill to Review

Communicate With Parents

Recruit parent assistance by locating the appropriate parent letter (pages 102–120), making copies, and sending the letter home.

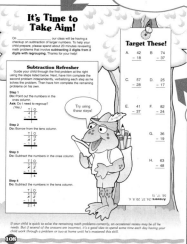

Problems for Practice

Subtraction Review for Parents

It's Time to Take Aim!

Target These!

Subtraction Refresher

2

Assess Student Understanding

Assess students' progress with student checkups (mini tests) on pages 103–121. Choose Checkup A or Checkup B.

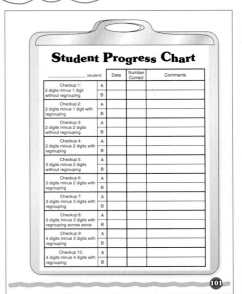

Checkup 4

Name _____ Date _____

A.	51 − 14	95 − 56	72 − 39	44 − 15	63 − 58
B.	86 − 57	22 − 16	64 − 29	51 − 27	37 − 18
C.	85 − 47	71 − 53	43 − 25	64 − 38	92 − 67
D.	58 − 39	33 − 29	64 − 17	72 − 28	73 − 46
E.	91 − 45	74 − 16	83 − 37	27 − 19	95 − 38

Test A: 2 digits minus 2 digits with regrouping

Checkup 4

Name _____ Date _____

A.	74 − 65	63 − 27	51 − 25	32 − 13	95 − 56
B.	58 − 49	41 − 19	84 − 67	86 − 39	42 − 27
C.	63 − 46	25 − 19	74 − 48	51 − 28	93 − 15
D.	93 − 74	82 − 15	36 − 28	63 − 34	24 − 16
E.	71 − 46	97 − 28	44 − 19	52 − 34	81 − 23

Test B: 2 digits minus 2 digits with regrouping

Two Checkups for Each Skill

Document Progress

Documenting student progress can be as easy as 1, 2, 3! Do the following for each student:
1. Make a copy of the student progress chart (page 101).
2. File the chart in his math portfolio or a class notebook.
3. Record the date each checkup is given, the number of correct answers, and any comments regarding the student's progress.

Student Progress Chart

(student)		Date	Number Correct	Comments
Checkup 1: 2 digits minus 1 digit without regrouping	A			
	B			
Checkup 2: 2 digits minus 1 digit with regrouping	A			
	B			
Checkup 3: 2 digits minus 2 digits without regrouping	A			
	B			
Checkup 4: 2 digits minus 2 digits with regrouping	A			
	B			
Checkup 5: 3 digits minus 2 digits without regrouping	A			
	B			
Checkup 6: 3 digits minus 2 digits with regrouping	A			
	B			
Checkup 7: 3 digits minus 3 digits with regrouping	A			
	B			
Checkup 8: 3 digits minus 3 digits with regrouping across zeros	A			
	B			
Checkup 9: 4 digits minus 3 digits with regrouping	A			
	B			
Checkup 10: 4 digits minus 4 digits with regrouping	A			
	B			

101

Celebrate!

Celebrate subtraction success using the awards on page 124.

Bull's-eye! Your subtraction skills have hit the target!

Student _____

Teacher _____

Date _____

Books in the Target Math Success series include

- *Basic Addition Facts to 18*
- *Basic Subtraction Facts to 18*
- *Addition of Larger Numbers*
- *Subtraction of Larger Numbers*
- *Basic Multiplication Facts and More*
- *Basic Division Facts and More*
- *Multiplication of Larger Numbers*
- *Division of Larger Numbers*
- *Fractions*
- *Decimals*

Managing Editor: Hope H. Taylor
Editor at Large: Diane Badden
Staff Editors: Kelly Coder, Kelli L. Gowdy, Deborah G. Swider
Copy Editors: Tazmen Carlisle, Amy Kirtley-Hill, Karen L. Mayworth, Kristy Parton, Debbie Shoffner, Cathy Edwards Simrell
Cover Artist: Kimberly Richard
Art Coordinator: Pam Crane
Artists: Pam Crane, Shane Freeman, Theresa Lewis Goode, Clevell Harris, Ivy L. Koonce, Clint Moore, Greg D. Rieves, Rebecca Saunders, Barry Slate, Stuart Smith, Donna K. Teal
The Mailbox® Books.com: Judy P. Wyndham (MANAGER); Jennifer Tipton Bennett (DESIGNER/ARTIST); Karen White (INTERNET COORDINATOR); Paul Fleetwood, Xiaoyun Wu (SYSTEMS)

President, The Mailbox Book Company™: Joseph C. Bucci
Director of Book Planning and Development: Chris Poindexter
Curriculum Director: Karen P. Shelton
Book Development Managers: Cayce Guiliano, Elizabeth H. Lindsay, Thad McLaurin
Editorial Planning: Kimberley Bruck (MANAGER); Debra Liverman, Sharon Murphy, Susan Walker (TEAM LEADERS)
Editorial and Freelance Management: Karen A. Brudnak; Sarah Hamblet, Hope Rodgers (EDITORIAL ASSISTANTS)
Editorial Production: Lisa K. Pitts (TRAFFIC MANAGER); Lynette Dickerson (TYPE SYSTEMS); Mark Rainey (TYPESETTER)
Librarian: Dorothy C. McKinney

www.themailbox.com

Subtraction of Larger Numbers

Subtraction of Larger Numbers
Table of Contents

Parent Communication and Student Checkups

*See pages 102–121 for corresponding parent communications and student checkups (mini tests) for these skills.

Rub-a-dub-dub

Name _____   Date _____

Subtract.
Color the bubble with the matching answer.

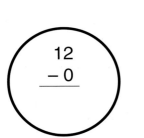

12
− 0

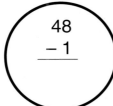

48
− 1

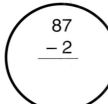

87
− 2

24
− 3

64
− 2

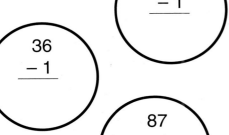

72
− 1

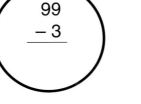

99
− 3

55
− 4

19
− 8

36
− 1

87
− 4

38
− 6

26
− 4

57
− 7

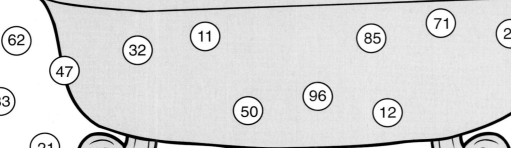

62 47 83 21 32 11 50 96 12 85 71 22 35 51

2 digits minus 1 digit without regrouping

7

Race to the Finish

Name _____ Date _____

Subtract.

36
− 5

49
− 3

17
− 4

85
− 1

64
− 2

57
− 2

76
− 4

28
− 6

18
− 3

45
− 2

92
− 1

29
− 6

88
− 4

53
− 1

8 **2 digits minus 1 digit without regrouping**

Turn Up the Tunes!

Name _____ Date _____

Subtract.

What do you get when you cross a radio with a refrigerator?

75 − 3 A	68 − 6 U	46 − 2 E
59 − 4 M	13 − 2 R	37 − 2 S
82 − 1 O	48 − 5 I	24 − 3 L
35 − 2 C	93 − 1 Y	67 − 4 L
76 − 2 C	57 − 5 L	88 − 3 O

To solve the riddle, match the letters to the numbered lines below.

___ ___ ___ ___ ___ ___   ___ ___ ___ ___   ___ ___ ___ ___ ___ !
11 44 72 52 63 92   33 81 85 21   55 62 35 43 74

2 digits minus 1 digit without regrouping

Fly Away Home

Name _____   Date _____

Subtract.
Help Lilly find her way home.
If the answer has a difference of less than 50, color the box red.

39 − 4	56 − 5	63 − 3	84 − 2	75 − 2
42 − 1	78 − 6	17 − 1	29 − 2	36 − 1
18 − 6	93 − 1	35 − 2	69 − 7	28 − 2
46 − 4	14 − 0	27 − 3	88 − 4	45 − 4

Ladybug Lane

2 digits minus 1 digit without regrouping

Penguins on Ice

Name _____ Date _____

Read.
Solve.
Show your work.

Petey spins 37 times on the ice. Patty spins 2 times. How many more times does Petey spin?

_____ spins

Peanut dives 59 times during the show. Pop dives 6 times. How many more times does Peanut dive?

_____ dives

On Monday, 76 penguins watched the show. On Tuesday, 5 penguins watched. How many more penguins watched on Monday?

_____ penguins

Patty skates for 45 minutes. Peanut skates for 3 minutes. How much longer does Patty skate?

_____ minutes

68 penguins wave red scarves during the show. 6 penguins wave blue scarves. How many more penguins wave red scarves?

_____ penguins

After the show, Petey eats 27 fish. Peanut eats 2 fish. How many more fish does Petey eat?

_____ fish

Keeping a Lookout

Name _____ Date _____

Subtract.
Show your work.

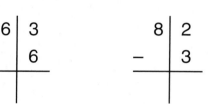

4 7	8 4	2 5
− 8	− 6	− 8

6 3	8 2	5 1
− 6	− 3	− 4

9 7	5 6	1 1
− 9	− 8	− 3

7 5	3 4	1 6
− 6	− 7	− 8

8 3	6 2
− 4	− 5

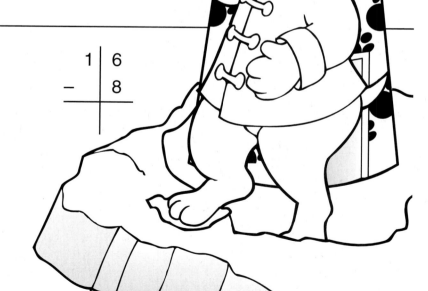

Art in Motion

Name _____ Date _____

Subtract.
Show your work.
Color by the code.

$$84 - 7$$

$$81 - 8$$

$$73 - 6$$

$$43 - 9$$

$$52 - 7$$

$$18 - 9$$

$$96 - 7$$

$$47 - 9$$

$$75 - 6$$

$$64 - 5$$

$$41 - 5$$

$$35 - 9$$

$$24 - 7$$

$$92 - 4$$

$$86 - 8$$

$$98 - 9$$

Color Code
0–35 = yellow
36–65 = red
66–95 = blue

2 digits minus 1 digit with regrouping

Soaring Over the Bar

Name _____   Date _____

Subtract.
Show your work.
Cross off the answer.

24 − 7	65 − 6	43 − 8	96 − 9
57 − 8	98 − 9	25 − 7	72 − 4
75 − 7	31 − 4	86 − 8	54 − 9
82 − 6	27 − 9	63 − 5	45 − 8

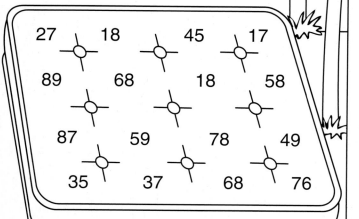

27   18   45   17

89   68   18   58

87   59   78   49

35   37   68   76

So Many Seashells

Name _____   Date _____

Subtract.
Show your work on another sheet of paper.
If the answer is correct, color the seashell.

85
− 6
89

46
− 8
38

24
− 7
27

65
− 9
56

74
− 7
67

35
− 8
27

92
− 4
88

74
− 6
69

52
− 3
59

83
− 6
77

27
− 9
18

52
− 5
57

45
− 7
38

37
− 8
39

62
− 6
56

93
− 4
89

2 digits minus 1 digit with regrouping

To Market, to Market

Name _____   Date _____

Read.
Solve.
Show your work.

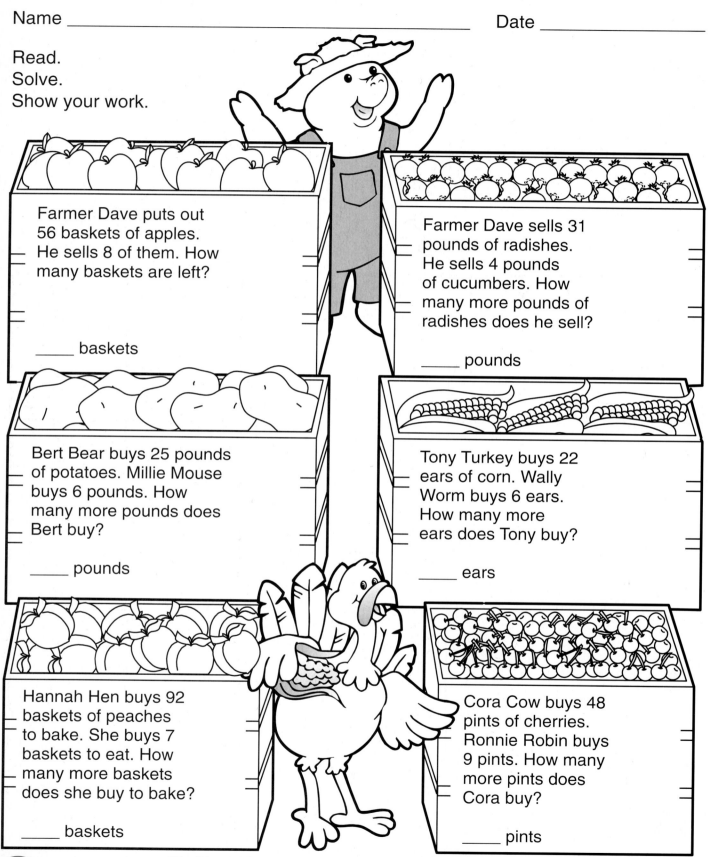

Farmer Dave puts out 56 baskets of apples. He sells 8 of them. How many baskets are left?

_____ baskets

Farmer Dave sells 31 pounds of radishes. He sells 4 pounds of cucumbers. How many more pounds of radishes does he sell?

_____ pounds

Bert Bear buys 25 pounds of potatoes. Millie Mouse buys 6 pounds. How many more pounds does Bert buy?

_____ pounds

Tony Turkey buys 22 ears of corn. Wally Worm buys 6 ears. How many more ears does Tony buy?

_____ ears

Hannah Hen buys 92 baskets of peaches to bake. She buys 7 baskets to eat. How many more baskets does she buy to bake?

_____ baskets

Cora Cow buys 48 pints of cherries. Ronnie Robin buys 9 pints. How many more pints does Cora buy?

_____ pints

Doing the Burger Boogie

Name _____ Date _____

Subtract.
Show your work.

Where do hamburgers go when they want to dance?

38 − 6	93 − 1	26 − 8	45 − 2	63 − 6	37 − 2
Y	**E**	**O**	**H**	**M**	**G**
24 − 7	87 − 4	73 − 6	76 − 4	64 − 2	45 − 8
H	**T**	**T**	**A**	**O**	**B**
88 − 3	75 − 7	49 − 3	96 − 9	31 − 4	57 − 5
E	**A**	**L**	**E**	**L**	**T**

To solve the riddle above, match the letters to the numbered lines below.

___ ___ ___ ___   ___ ___   ___ ___   ___ ___ ___   ___ ___ ___ ___   ___ ___ ___ ___
67 17 92 32   35 62   67 18   52 43 87   57 85 68 83   37 72 27 46

Gumball Surprises

Name _____   Date _____

Subtract.
Color the gumball with the matching answer.

54 − 31	38 − 16
75 − 40	26 − 15
69 − 42	85 − 32
32 − 11	74 − 53
57 − 27	25 − 12

93 − 62	49 − 17	67 − 31	74 − 22

2 digits minus 2 digits without regrouping

Shoe Shopping Spree

Name _____   Date _____

Help the chickens get to the shoe store.
Circle each correct fact.
Draw a line to connect the circled facts.

$$\begin{array}{r} 47 \\ -31 \\ \hline 16 \end{array}$$

$$\begin{array}{r} 28 \\ -14 \\ \hline 14 \end{array}$$

$$\begin{array}{r} 32 \\ -12 \\ \hline 21 \end{array}$$

$$\begin{array}{r} 57 \\ -33 \\ \hline 25 \end{array}$$

$$\begin{array}{r} 24 \\ -10 \\ \hline 34 \end{array}$$

$$\begin{array}{r} 98 \\ -16 \\ \hline 82 \end{array}$$

$$\begin{array}{r} 85 \\ -42 \\ \hline 43 \end{array}$$

$$\begin{array}{r} 42 \\ -11 \\ \hline 53 \end{array}$$

$$\begin{array}{r} 36 \\ -25 \\ \hline 21 \end{array}$$

$$\begin{array}{r} 45 \\ -33 \\ \hline 12 \end{array}$$

$$\begin{array}{r} 75 \\ -14 \\ \hline 61 \end{array}$$

$$\begin{array}{r} 59 \\ -26 \\ \hline 33 \end{array}$$

$$\begin{array}{r} 79 \\ -19 \\ \hline 98 \end{array}$$

$$\begin{array}{r} 86 \\ -36 \\ \hline 52 \end{array}$$

$$\begin{array}{r} 93 \\ -72 \\ \hline 21 \end{array}$$

$$\begin{array}{r} 65 \\ -52 \\ \hline 13 \end{array}$$

$$\begin{array}{r} 46 \\ -15 \\ \hline 21 \end{array}$$

$$\begin{array}{r} 74 \\ -41 \\ \hline 22 \end{array}$$

$$\begin{array}{r} 87 \\ -60 \\ \hline 17 \end{array}$$

$$\begin{array}{r} 29 \\ -16 \\ \hline 13 \end{array}$$

$$\begin{array}{r} 95 \\ -13 \\ \hline 88 \end{array}$$

$$\begin{array}{r} 58 \\ -42 \\ \hline 15 \end{array}$$

SHOE BUSINESS

Annual
Shoe
Sale

2 digits minus 2 digits without regrouping   **19**

Schooltime Jive

Name _____   Date _____

Subtract.
Color by the code.

$$67 - 52$$

$$69 - 32$$

$$88 - 61$$

$$96 - 56$$

$$49 - 20$$

$$69 - 43$$

$$78 - 68$$

$$54 - 13$$

$$57 - 27$$

$$99 - 81$$

$$37 - 13$$

$$45 - 13$$

$$75 - 54$$

$$86 - 42$$

Dragons Rule!

Name _____ Date _____

Subtract.
Cross off a matching answer.

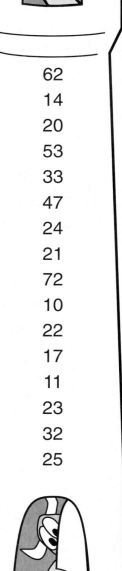

31 − 20	90 − 70	97 − 50	67 − 42
47 − 14	86 − 76	79 − 58	35 − 12
49 − 35	54 − 22	67 − 43	28 − 11
99 − 27	38 − 16	74 − 21	85 − 23

62
14
20
53
33
47
24
21
72
10
22
17
11
23
32
25

Home Improvements

Name _____ Date _____

Read.
Solve.
Show your work.

The bugs buy 35 gallons of paint. They use 21. How many gallons are left?

_____ gallons

The bugs have 54 brushes. They use 23. How many brushes are left? _____ brushes	The bugs buy 46 paint pans. 10 crack. How many pans are not cracked? _____ pans
There are 27 bugs painting. 14 go home. How many bugs are left? _____ bugs	The bugs carry 27 paint cans up the ladder. 13 spill. How many cans did not spill? _____ cans
The bugs use 29 paint rollers. 12 break. How many rollers are not broken? _____ rollers	

Computer Solutions

Name _____   Date _____

Subtract.
Show your work.

```
  7 3          3 5          9 6          5 8          4 2
- 4 6        - 2 7        - 3 8        - 2 9        - 3 7
```

```
  2 6          6 1          2 4          5 2          8 5
- 1 9        - 2 5        - 1 8        - 3 7        - 5 9
```

```
  9 4          4 7          8 1          7 3          3 5
- 6 7        - 2 8        - 4 3        - 3 8        - 1 6
```

Stargazers

Name _____   Date _____

Subtract.
Show your work.
Color the star with the matching answer.

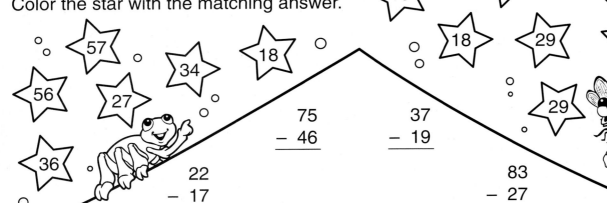

75 − 46	37 − 19
22 − 17	83 − 27

37 − 18	51 − 22	72 − 34	65 − 29
84 − 68	56 − 29	45 − 18	74 − 56
45 − 18	93 − 36	66 − 37	52 − 18

Stars: 16, 27, 38, 29, 18, 29, 19, 29, 27, 5, 57, 34, 18, 56, 27, 36

Pond Pals

Name _____   Date _____

Subtract.
Show your work.
Connect the dots in order from
    least to greatest.

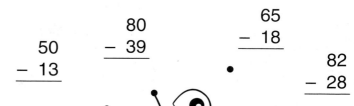

$$50 - 13$$

$$80 - 39$$

$$65 - 18$$

$$82 - 28$$

$$74 - 38$$

$$82 - 48$$

$$95 - 36$$

$$53 - 24$$

$$84 - 19$$

$$87 - 69$$

$$95 - 6$$

$$60 - 34$$

$$90 - 22$$

$$93 - 8$$

$$92 - 18$$

$$93 - 17$$

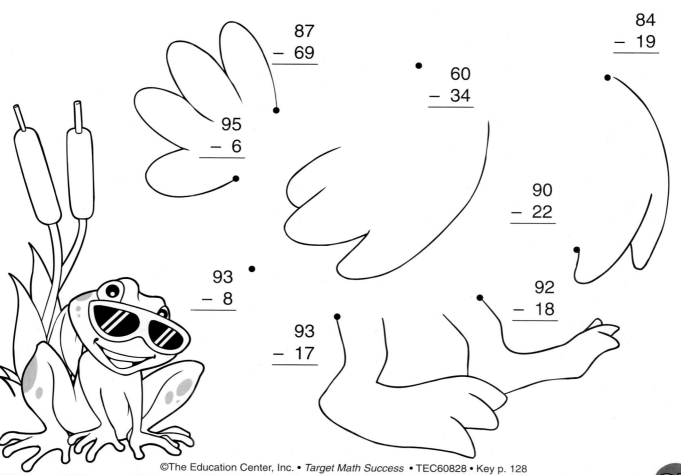

2 digits minus 2 digits with regrouping

Movie Munchies

Name _____   Date _____

Subtract.
Show your work.
Help Gus find his soda.
Color each popcorn tub with an even difference yellow.

95 − 36	27 − 18	40 − 11	98 − 49
60 − 24	51 − 27	30 − 12	83 − 26
32 − 19	74 − 17	43 − 25	52 − 35
87 − 48	91 − 24	75 − 37	60 − 18

50
− 25

64
− 29

A Good Day for Golf

Name _____ Date _____

Read.
Subtract.
Show your work.

Oscar's score is 92. Ollie's is 79. How many more points does Oscar score than Ollie?

_____ points

Opal brings 55 hats to give the golfers. She gives away 19 of them. How many hats are left?

_____ hats

Oliver plays 34 holes. Olivia plays 17. How many more holes does Oliver play than Olivia?

_____ holes

Ollie buys 62 golf balls in the gift shop. Opal buys 43. How many more balls does Ollie buy?

_____ balls

Olivia's bag weighs 50 pounds. Oscar's weighs 39 pounds. How much more does Olivia's bag weigh than Oscar's?

_____ pounds

Oliver drives his golf cart 75 miles. Opal drives hers 28 miles. How many more miles does Oliver drive than Opal?

_____ miles

Picture-Perfect?

Name _____   Date _____

Subtract.
Show your work on another sheet of paper.
If the answer is correct, color the photograph.

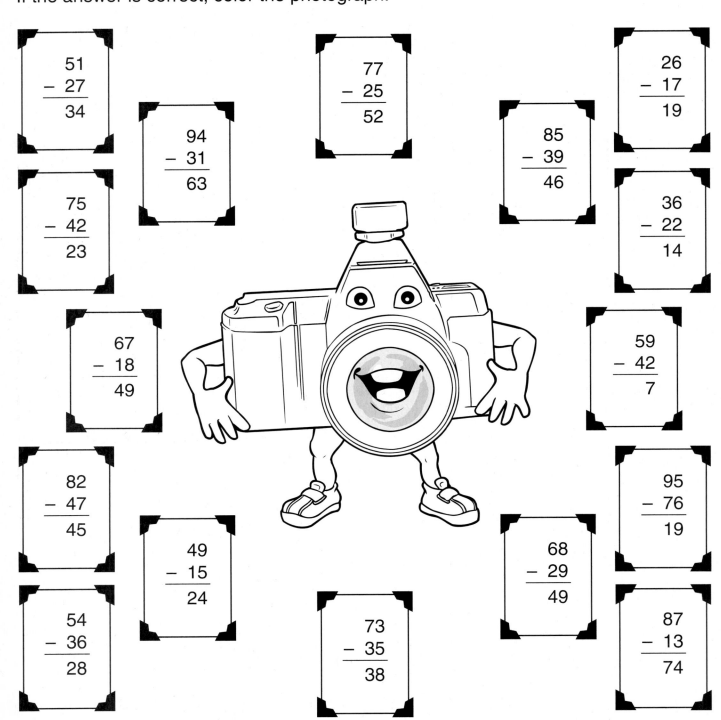

$$\begin{array}{r} 51 \\ -\ 27 \\ \hline 34 \end{array}$$

$$\begin{array}{r} 94 \\ -\ 31 \\ \hline 63 \end{array}$$

$$\begin{array}{r} 77 \\ -\ 25 \\ \hline 52 \end{array}$$

$$\begin{array}{r} 26 \\ -\ 17 \\ \hline 19 \end{array}$$

$$\begin{array}{r} 75 \\ -\ 42 \\ \hline 23 \end{array}$$

$$\begin{array}{r} 85 \\ -\ 39 \\ \hline 46 \end{array}$$

$$\begin{array}{r} 36 \\ -\ 22 \\ \hline 14 \end{array}$$

$$\begin{array}{r} 67 \\ -\ 18 \\ \hline 49 \end{array}$$

$$\begin{array}{r} 59 \\ -\ 42 \\ \hline 7 \end{array}$$

$$\begin{array}{r} 82 \\ -\ 47 \\ \hline 45 \end{array}$$

$$\begin{array}{r} 95 \\ -\ 76 \\ \hline 19 \end{array}$$

$$\begin{array}{r} 49 \\ -\ 15 \\ \hline 24 \end{array}$$

$$\begin{array}{r} 68 \\ -\ 29 \\ \hline 49 \end{array}$$

$$\begin{array}{r} 54 \\ -\ 36 \\ \hline 28 \end{array}$$

$$\begin{array}{r} 73 \\ -\ 35 \\ \hline 38 \end{array}$$

$$\begin{array}{r} 87 \\ -\ 13 \\ \hline 74 \end{array}$$

Darting Dragonflies

Name _____   Date _____

Subtract.
Show your work.
Color each space with an
    even difference.

Dragonflies are the
fastest insects. How
many miles per hour
do they fly?

Let's Eat!

Name _____ Date _____

Subtract.
Circle each matching answer in the picture.

| 563 | 279 | 421 | 386 | 575 |
| − 41 | − 58 | − 10 | − 42 | − 34 |

| 671 | 297 | 654 | 383 | 294 |
| − 20 | − 44 | − 32 | − 21 | − 62 |

| 197 | 460 | 730 | 125 | 615 |
| − 31 | − 20 | − 20 | − 12 | − 13 |

3 digits minus 2 digits without regrouping

Unwinding at the Web

Name _____   Date _____

Subtract.
Color by the code.

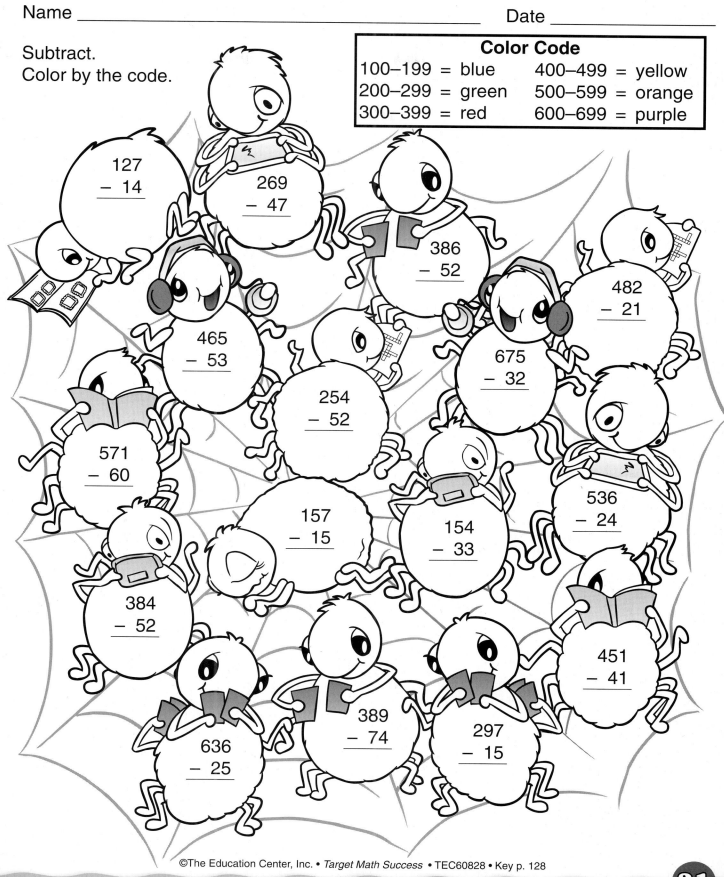

127
− 14

269
− 47

386
− 52

482
− 21

465
− 53

254
− 52

675
− 32

571
− 60

157
− 15

154
− 33

536
− 24

384
− 52

451
− 41

636
− 25

389
− 74

297
− 15

Shootin' Hoops

Name _____ Date _____

Subtract.

427 − 13 B	651 − 30 T	175 − 22 U	295 − 74 O	562 − 30 H	385 − 44 L	721 − 20 E
965 − 42 E	458 − 31 B	634 − 23 E	879 − 48 L	275 − 31 A	994 − 62 H	647 − 25 G
397 − 46 C	625 − 15 Y	284 − 61 A	798 − 57 H			
179 − 46 S	545 − 43 E	886 − 43 T				

Why can't you play basketball with pigs?
To solve the riddle, match the letters to the numbered lines below.

___ ___ ___ ___ ___ ___ ___   ___ ___ ___ ___
414 502 351 244 153 133 923   621 532 701 610

                                                          !

___ ___ ___   ___ ___ ___   ___ ___ ___ ___
932 221 622   843 741 611   427 223 831 341

©The Education Center, Inc. • *Target Math Success* • TEC60828 • Key p. 128

3 digits minus 2 digits without regrouping

Look Whooo's at the Library!

Name _____ Date _____

Subtract.
Color by the code.

$$827 - 14$$

$$465 - 30$$

$$384 - 63$$

$$270 - 30$$

$$135 - 23$$

$$973 - 31$$

$$194 - 32$$

$$684 - 61$$

$$265 - 14$$

$$378 - 64$$

$$929 - 16$$

$$593 - 33$$

$$524 - 13$$

$$279 - 25$$

$$166 - 25$$

$$464 - 42$$

$$637 - 25$$

$$758 - 31$$

$$842 - 10$$

$$954 - 22$$

Leo's Sweet Treats

Name _____ Date _____

Read.
Solve.
Show your work.

Leo has 178 gumdrops. He sells 46. How many gumdrops are left? _____ gumdrops	There are 256 suckers on a tray. Leo moves 35 to a jar. How many suckers are left on the tray? _____ suckers
Leo sells 454 chocolates on Monday. That is 21 more than he sells on Tuesday. How many chocolates does he sell on Tuesday? _____ chocolates	Leo has 748 caramels. 26 melt. How many caramels are left? _____ caramels
Leo sells 672 sour balls and 51 gumdrops. How many more sour balls does he sell? _____ sour balls	Leo has 497 jelly beans. 84 are red and the rest are green. How many jelly beans are green? _____ green

Excellent Exercise!

Name _____ Date _____

Subtract.

 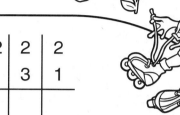

	1	9	0
−		2	5

	2	2	2
−		3	1

	3	6	3
−		5	4

	1	7	5
−		8	3

	3	4	6
−		9	4

	4	2	8
−		1	9

	2	5	4
−		9	3

	5	3	6
−		5	2

	1	6	8
−		7	0

	4	3	5
−		8	1

	3	3	3
−		6	2

	5	1	8
−		2	5

	2	6	1
−		9	1

	3	0	3
−		6	1

3 digits minus 2 digits with one regrouping

Paulie Wants a Pizza!

Name _____ Date _____

Subtract.
Cross off the answer.

334
118
170
474
509
Paulie

Paulie's Pizzeria

$$\begin{array}{r} 549 \\ -98 \\ \hline \end{array} \qquad \begin{array}{r} 491 \\ -63 \\ \hline \end{array}$$

$$\begin{array}{r} 347 \\ -60 \\ \hline \end{array} \qquad \begin{array}{r} 529 \\ -55 \\ \hline \end{array} \qquad \begin{array}{r} 418 \\ -88 \\ \hline \end{array}$$

$$\begin{array}{r} 325 \\ -34 \\ \hline \end{array} \qquad \begin{array}{r} 534 \\ -18 \\ \hline \end{array} \qquad \begin{array}{r} 462 \\ -71 \\ \hline \end{array} \qquad \begin{array}{r} 276 \\ -84 \\ \hline \end{array}$$

$$\begin{array}{r} 284 \\ -57 \\ \hline \end{array} \qquad \begin{array}{r} 325 \\ -93 \\ \hline \end{array} \qquad \begin{array}{r} 183 \\ -65 \\ \hline \end{array} \qquad \begin{array}{r} 279 \\ -94 \\ \hline \end{array} \qquad \begin{array}{r} 231 \\ -61 \\ \hline \end{array}$$

185	192	330
287	528	451
232	516	391
350	291	
428	227	

$$\begin{array}{r} 556 \\ -28 \\ \hline \end{array} \qquad \begin{array}{r} 437 \\ -87 \\ \hline \end{array} \qquad \begin{array}{r} 568 \\ -59 \\ \hline \end{array} \qquad \begin{array}{r} 353 \\ -19 \\ \hline \end{array}$$

3 digits minus 2 digits with one regrouping

Fun Fishing Buddies

Name _____ Date _____

Subtract.
Help Frank find his fishing buddy.
Use a green crayon to color each box
  with a difference of less than 100.

171 − 90	452 − 17	326 − 81	283 − 19	145 − 26
149 − 61	168 − 49	236 − 17	469 − 95	391 − 22
678 − 82	136 − 75	157 − 84	143 − 52	284 − 39
439 − 67	541 − 36	318 − 97	122 − 40	175 − 82

The Ice-Cream Counter

Name _____ Date _____

Read.
Solve.
Show your work.

Bessie

The jar has 396 sprinkles.
Bessie uses 27 sprinkles.
How many sprinkles are left?

_____ sprinkles

Bessie leaves 428 ice-cream
sandwiches by the window. 36
of them melt. How many ice-
cream sandwiches are left?

_____ ice-cream sandwiches

The store has 564 ice-cream
cones. Bessie uses 35 cones
in one day. How many cones
are left?

_____ cones

Bessie makes 473 gallons
of ice cream. She sells 91
gallons. How many gallons
are left?

_____ gallons

Bessie makes 681 milk
shakes in a month. 72 of the
milk shakes are vanilla. How
many are not vanilla?

_____ milk shakes

Bessie has 835 jars of hot
fudge. She uses 41 of them.
How many jars of hot fudge
are left?

_____ jars

Make a Wish

Name _____ Date _____

Subtract.
Show your work.

```
  9 | 6 | 2        3 | 4 | 5        6 | 3 | 5        7 | 7 | 3
-     | 8 | 5    -     | 8 | 9    -     | 9 | 8    -     | 8 | 6
```

```
  6 | 2 | 1        5 | 6 | 3        8 | 4 | 0        2 | 5 | 4
-     | 3 | 6    -     | 7 | 4    -     | 7 | 7    -     | 6 | 7
```

```
  9 | 4 | 0        4 | 3 | 2        7 | 6 | 1        3 | 2 | 7
-     | 6 | 3    -     | 7 | 7    -     | 9 | 4    -     | 4 | 9
```

```
  5 | 5 | 3        5 | 7 | 6
-     | 8 | 8    -     | 8 | 7
```

Moving Day

Name _____   Date _____

Subtract.
Show your work.

$$\begin{array}{r} 563 \\ -\ \ 86 \\ \hline \end{array}$$

$$\begin{array}{r} 780 \\ -\ \ 98 \\ \hline \end{array}$$

$$\begin{array}{r} 757 \\ -\ \ 79 \\ \hline \end{array}$$

$$\begin{array}{r} 424 \\ -\ \ 48 \\ \hline \end{array}$$

$$\begin{array}{r} 245 \\ -\ \ 59 \\ \hline \end{array}$$

$$\begin{array}{r} 231 \\ -\ \ 87 \\ \hline \end{array}$$

$$\begin{array}{r} 980 \\ -\ \ 95 \\ \hline \end{array}$$

$$\begin{array}{r} 317 \\ -\ \ 38 \\ \hline \end{array}$$

$$\begin{array}{r} 876 \\ -\ \ 97 \\ \hline \end{array}$$

$$\begin{array}{r} 542 \\ -\ \ 74 \\ \hline \end{array}$$

$$\begin{array}{r} 160 \\ -\ \ 87 \\ \hline \end{array}$$

$$\begin{array}{r} 614 \\ -\ \ 46 \\ \hline \end{array}$$

$$\begin{array}{r} 428 \\ -\ \ 49 \\ \hline \end{array}$$

$$\begin{array}{r} 651 \\ -\ \ 84 \\ \hline \end{array}$$

$$\begin{array}{r} 335 \\ -\ \ 78 \\ \hline \end{array}$$

Light Up the Night!

Name _____ Date _____

Subtract.
Show your work on another sheet of paper.
If the answer is correct, color the burst red.

$$\begin{array}{r} 750 \\ -\ 73 \\ \hline 677 \end{array}$$

$$\begin{array}{r} 447 \\ -\ 89 \\ \hline 368 \end{array}$$

$$\begin{array}{r} 584 \\ -\ 96 \\ \hline 488 \end{array}$$

$$\begin{array}{r} 118 \\ -\ 39 \\ \hline 69 \end{array}$$

$$\begin{array}{r} 621 \\ -\ 55 \\ \hline 566 \end{array}$$

$$\begin{array}{r} 135 \\ -\ 88 \\ \hline 47 \end{array}$$

$$\begin{array}{r} 260 \\ -\ 72 \\ \hline 188 \end{array}$$

$$\begin{array}{r} 352 \\ -\ 66 \\ \hline 296 \end{array}$$

$$\begin{array}{r} 386 \\ -\ 97 \\ \hline 309 \end{array}$$

$$\begin{array}{r} 970 \\ -\ 84 \\ \hline 886 \end{array}$$

$$\begin{array}{r} 421 \\ -\ 39 \\ \hline 388 \end{array}$$

$$\begin{array}{r} 640 \\ -\ 67 \\ \hline 573 \end{array}$$

$$\begin{array}{r} 865 \\ -\ 79 \\ \hline 784 \end{array}$$

$$\begin{array}{r} 334 \\ -\ 57 \\ \hline 277 \end{array}$$

$$\begin{array}{r} 513 \\ -\ 25 \\ \hline 478 \end{array}$$

$$\begin{array}{r} 577 \\ -\ 98 \\ \hline 469 \end{array}$$

©The Education Center, Inc. • *Target Math Success* • TEC60828 • Key p. 129

Assorted Chocolates

Name _____   Date _____

Read.
Solve.
Show your work.

CANDY
MACHINE

In the morning, the workers make 435 chocolate-covered cherries. In the afternoon, they make 68. How many more do they make in the morning?

_____ chocolate-covered cherries

On Monday, the workers make 710 chocolate bars. On Tuesday, they make 47. How many more do they make on Monday?

_____ bars

Each year, the workers must make 821 boxes of coconut bars. During January, they make 75. How many boxes are left?

_____ boxes

Every week, the workers make 646 bags of chocolate chips. They also make 58 bags of chocolate chunks. How many more bags of chocolate chips do they make?

_____ bags of chocolate chips

For Valentine's Day, the workers prepare 273 heart-shaped boxes. They ship 96 boxes right away. How many boxes are left?

_____ boxes

On Thursday, the workers make 230 almond bars. On Friday, they ship 92 almond bars. How many are left?

_____ bars

Digging Up Diamonds

Name _____ Date _____

Subtract.
Circle the answers that are odd.
Connect the circled answers to help
    Grover find the diamonds.

$$175 - 82$$

$$760 - 13$$ $$462 - 77$$

$$275 - 93$$

$$986 - 35$$ $$335 - 21$$

$$610 - 28$$

$$492 - 55$$

$$440 - 62$$ $$847 - 18$$

$$351 - 82$$

$$578 - 64$$ $$795 - 87$$

$$665 - 34$$

$$839 - 51$$ $$182 - 54$$

3 digits minus 2 digits with and without regrouping

Perfectly Square

Name _____   Date _____

Subtract.
Show your work.
Use your answers to complete each number puzzle.

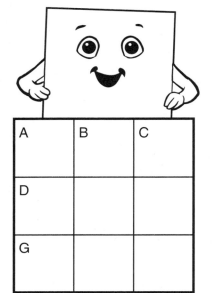

Across

A. 284
  − 42

D. 582
  − 19

E. 844
  − 97

Down

A. 320
  − 63

B. 516
  − 52

C. 253
  − 16

A	B	C
D		
G		

F	G	H
I		
J		

Across

F. 840
  − 46

I. 385
  − 52

J. 423
  − 75

Down

F. 815
  − 82

G. 975
  − 41

H. 497
  − 59

Across

K. 756
  − 24

N. 640
  − 78

O. 193
  − 47

Down

K. 850
  − 99

L. 389
  − 25

M. 317
  − 91

K	L	M
N		
O		

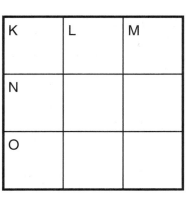

3 digits minus 2 digits with and without regrouping

What's for Lunch?

Name _____   Date _____

Subtract.
Color by the code.

485	643
− 230	− 413

375	728
− 165	− 526

618	999
− 318	− 600

767	560
− 334	− 110

560	439
− 360	− 217

994	799
− 773	− 501

898	787
− 540	− 412

676	989
− 275	− 501

Hamster Hideaway

Name _____ Date _____

Subtract.
Cross off the answer on the wheel.

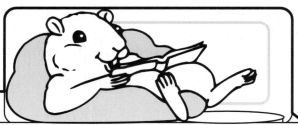

989 − 685	476 − 235	697 − 413	897 − 557	788 − 601

365
− 122

435 − 121	592 − 341	467 − 264	939 − 533	488 − 214

897
− 597

659
− 329

956
− 843

384
− 273

695
− 510

291
− 151

742
− 500

753
− 110

246
− 146

587
− 432

621
− 410

Wheel numbers: 243, 111, 274, 185, 100, 284, 187, 643, 330, 340, 241, 242, 155, 203, 304, 314, 113, 251, 406, 211, 140, 300

Running to the Oasis

Name _____   Date _____

Subtract.
Show your work on another sheet
  of paper.
Help Rudy Roadrunner find the oasis.
If the answer is correct, color the box.

$$986 - 871 = 115$$

$$716 - 315 = 401$$

$$349 - 222 = 127$$

$$574 - 260 = 314$$

$$329 - 125 = 204$$

$$640 - 540 = 180$$

$$651 - 540 = 311$$

$$681 - 431 = 250$$

$$980 - 360 = 620$$

$$249 - 138 = 211$$

$$268 - 135 = 133$$

$$234 - 103 = 131$$

$$365 - 124 = 241$$

$$731 - 410 = 321$$

$$235 - 134 = 131$$

$$624 - 311 = 413$$

$$438 - 338 = 100$$

$$718 - 506 = 312$$

$$537 - 216 = 121$$

$$421 - 320 = 100$$

$$856 - 432 = 424$$

Chew Toy

Name _____ Date _____

Subtract.
Color by the code.

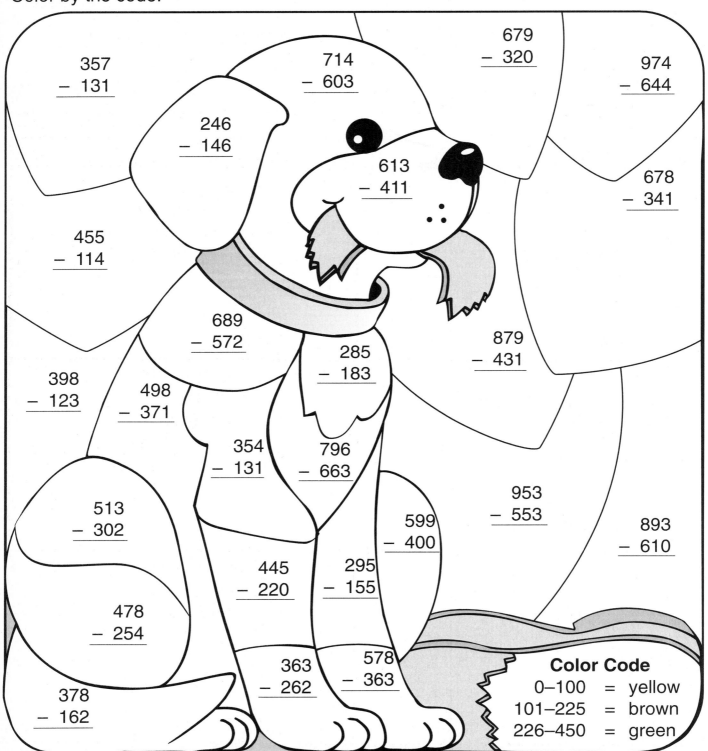

357
− 131

714
− 603

679
− 320

974
− 644

246
− 146

613
− 411

678
− 341

455
− 114

689
− 572

285
− 183

879
− 431

398
− 123

498
− 371

354
− 131

796
− 663

953
− 553

513
− 302

599
− 400

893
− 610

445
− 220

295
− 155

478
− 254

363
− 262

578
− 363

378
− 162

Color Code

0–100 = yellow
101–225 = brown
226–450 = green

3 digits minus 3 digits without regrouping

Lunch Line

Name _____ Date _____

Read.
Solve.
Show your work.

There are 683 seats in the lunchroom. 541 students sit in the lunchroom. How many seats are left?

_____ seats

The lunchroom has 578 lunches. 466 students buy their lunches. How many lunches are left?

_____ lunches

There are 425 trays in the lunchroom. 104 trays are orange. How many trays are not orange?

_____ trays

The milk cooler has 732 cartons of milk. 310 cartons are chocolate milk. How many cartons are not chocolate milk?

_____ cartons

The ice-cream cooler has 549 ice pops. 327 students buy ice pops. How many ice pops are left?

_____ ice pops

There are 978 napkins. The students use 612. How many napkins are left?

_____ napkins

Under the Big Top

Name _____   Date _____

Subtract.
Show your work.

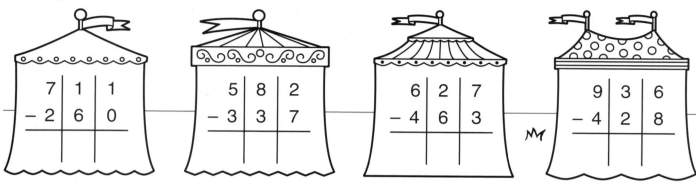

```
  7 1 1
- 2 6 0
```

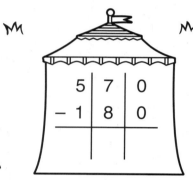
```
  5 8 2
- 3 3 7
```

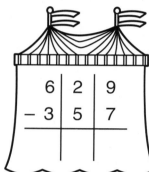
```
  6 2 7
- 4 6 3
```

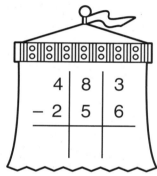
```
  9 3 6
- 4 2 8
```

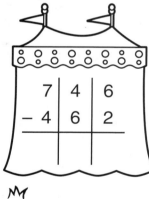
```
  2 6 4
- 1 5 9
```

```
  5 7 0
- 1 8 0
```

```
  6 2 9
- 3 5 7
```

```
  4 8 3
- 2 5 6
```

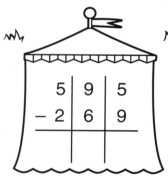
```
  7 4 6
- 4 6 2
```

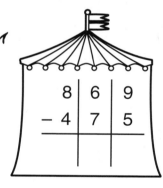
```
  5 9 5
- 2 6 9
```

```
  8 6 9
- 4 7 5
```

```
  7 9 8
- 5 3 9
```

3 digits minus 3 digits with one regrouping

Beaver on Board

Name _____   Date _____

Subtract.
Show your work.
Color by the code.

Color Code
100–200 = red
201–300 = blue
301–400 = yellow
401–600 = brown

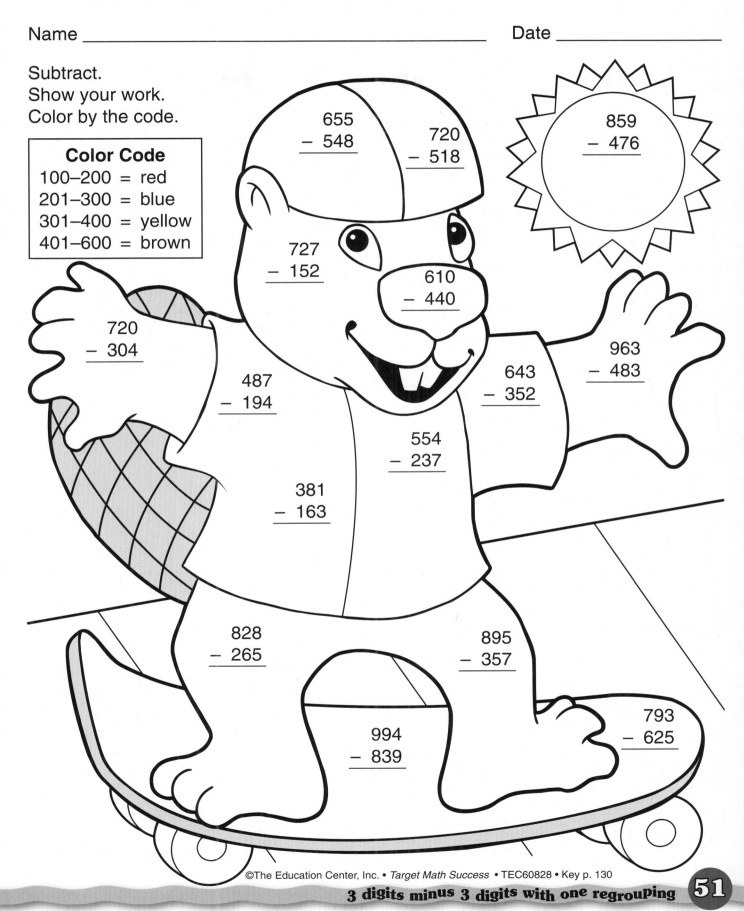

655
− 548

720
− 518

859
− 476

727
− 152

610
− 440

720
− 304

487
− 194

963
− 483

643
− 352

554
− 237

381
− 163

828
− 265

895
− 357

994
− 839

793
− 625

©The Education Center, Inc. • *Target Math Success* • TEC60828 • Key p. 130

3 digits minus 3 digits with one regrouping   51

Play Ball!

Name _____   Date _____

Subtract.
Show your work.

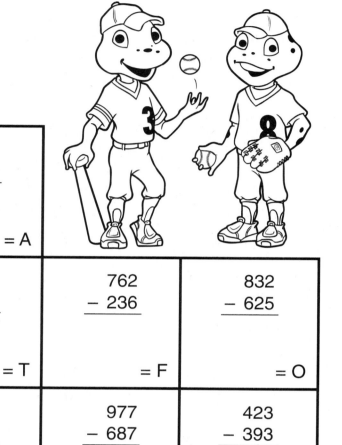

Why are frogs so good at baseball?

496 − 237 = E	251 − 233 = O	965 − 481 = A

674 − 439 = T	347 − 161 = L	529 − 272 = T	762 − 236 = F	832 − 625 = O
657 − 309 = E	768 − 671 = H	561 − 425 = F	977 − 687 = C	423 − 393 = Y
638 − 119 = T	983 − 854 = C	323 − 280 = H	494 − 158 = L	787 − 538 = A

882 − 724 = S	896 − 179 = I

To solve the riddle, match the letters to the numbered lines below.

___ ___ ___ ___   ___ ___ ___ ___ ___   ___
235 97 259 30   129 249 519 290 43   484

___ ___ ___   ___ ___   ___ ___ ___ ___ ___
186 207 257   18 136   526 336 717 348 158

©The Education Center, Inc. • *Target Math Success* • TEC60828 • Key p. 131

Lots of Lava

Name _____   Date _____

Subtract.
Show your work.
Color a matching answer.

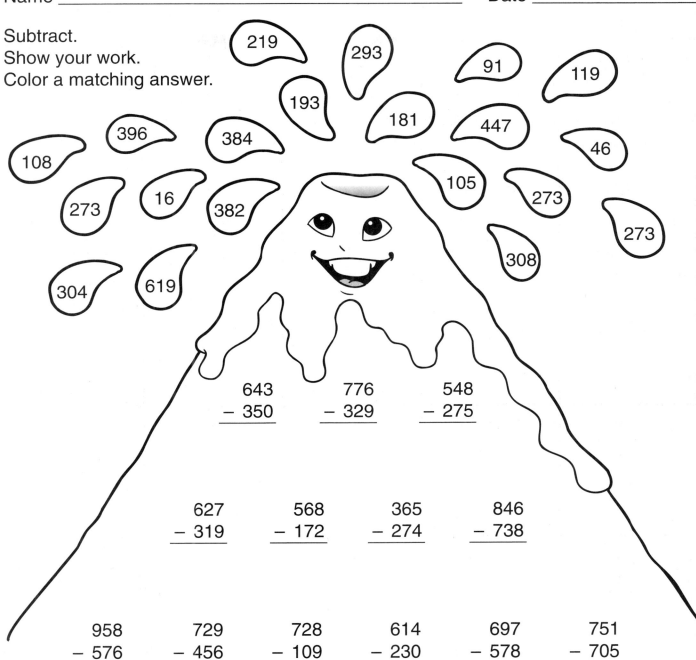

643
− 350

776
− 329

548
− 275

627
− 319

568
− 172

365
− 274

846
− 738

958
− 576

729
− 456

728
− 109

614
− 230

697
− 578

751
− 705

327
− 146

992
− 688

970
− 954

456
− 183

964
− 859

385
− 192

467
− 248

3 digits minus 3 digits with one regrouping

At the Museum

Name _____   Date _____

Read.
Solve.
Show your work.

There are 834 pictures.
272 have frames. The
rest do not. How many
pictures do not have
frames?

_____ pictures

The museum has 284
paintings. 109 are oil
paintings and the rest are
watercolor. How many
watercolor paintings are
there?

_____ watercolor paintings

There are 681 visitors
in the museum. 265
go home. How many
visitors are left?

_____ visitors

There are 559 statues
in the museum. 264 are
made of marble and the
rest are made of stone.
How many statues are
made of stone?

_____ stone statues

There are 723 paintings of
animals. 182 are of horses.
How many paintings are
not of horses?

_____ paintings

There are 712 steps in the
museum. If a visitor climbs
450 steps, how many are left?

_____ steps

©The Education Center, Inc. • *Target Math Success* • TEC60828 • Key p. 131

Story problems

Cactus Calculations

Name _____   Date _____

Subtract.
Show your work.

```
  4 5 7        3 2 0        6 1 4
- 1 6 9      - 2 8 6      - 3 3 7
```

```
  7 3 1        9 4 3        8 6 0        5 3 2
- 5 5 8      - 1 7 5      - 5 8 1      - 1 5 6
```

```
  6 7 0        2 5 5        5 7 3        8 4 7
- 5 9 4      - 1 9 8      - 3 8 6      - 7 6 8
```

```
  3 1 3        7 4 0        4 8 2        9 2 5
- 2 2 5      - 1 4 2      - 2 9 3      - 4 5 7
```

```
  8 3 7
- 6 7 9
```

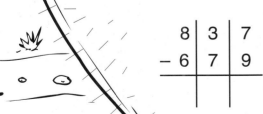

3 digits minus 3 digits with two regroupings 55

Pipin' Hot!

Name _____   Date _____

Subtract.
Show your work.

720
− 385

348
− 289

453
− 176

817
− 698

594
− 398

375
− 298

640
− 575

461
− 175

725
− 189

980
− 291

853
− 385

536
− 257

227
− 139

616
− 117

932
− 556

752
− 468

Birds on a Wire

Name _____   Date _____

Subtract.
Show your work.
Color by the code.

426
− 379

921
− 143

483
− 195

752
− 287

516
− 298

640
− 586

738
− 139

850
− 697

941
− 254

716
− 249

815
− 387

563
− 167

662
− 289

872
− 184

220
− 175

934
− 179

3 digits minus 3 digits with two regroupings

Just Ripe!

Name _____ Date _____

Subtract.
Show your work.
Color the apple with the matching answer.

910	318	624	823	570	743
− 722	− 169	− 456	− 686	− 183	− 397

762	651	480	517	831	457
− 675	− 259	− 391	− 338	− 486	− 279

214	582	375	745	260	936
− 148	− 284	− 278	− 549	− 167	− 897

School's in Session

Name _____   Date _____

Read.
Solve.
Show your work.

Seamore's Sea School

Seamore has 817 students in his school. Madame Mermaid has 639 students in her school. How many more students does Seamore have?

_____ students

Seamore ordered 394 new science books and 650 math books. How many more math books than science books were ordered?

_____ math books

At Seamore's school, there are 277 third graders and 361 second graders. How many more second graders than third graders attend the school?

_____ second graders

Seamore bought 689 new pencils for the students. 742 students came to school. How many more pencils does Seamore need?

_____ pencils

925 parents came to the open house. 468 students came with their parents. How many more parents than students were there?

_____ parents

195 students swim to school and 574 ride the underwater express. How many more students are riders than swimmers?

_____ riders

©The Education Center, Inc. • *Target Math Success* • TEC60828 • Key p. 131

Lounging Lobster

Name _____   Date _____

Subtract.
Show your work.
Color the music note with the correct answer.

```
   6 0 4        9 8 0        2 0 4        7 3 0
 - 2 5 7      - 4 2 3      - 1 1 8      - 3 9 2
```

```
   8 5 0        1 9 0        5 0 0        3 0 6
 - 6 3 2      - 1 7 4      - 2 9 7      - 1 3 8
```

```
   7 0 3        4 0 0        8 0 7        6 1 0
 - 5 4 6      - 3 6 9      - 3 1 4      - 5 7 6
```

```
   5 2 0        9 0 7
 - 4 5 5      - 5 8 1
```

```
   3 8 0
 - 2 4 7
```

Music notes: 157, 16, 557, 34, 347, 326, 31, 218, 86, 65, 203, 133, 338, 493, 168

3 digits minus 3 digits with regrouping across zeros

Up, Up, and Away

Name _____ Date _____

Subtract.
Show your work.
Color by the code.

$\begin{array}{r} 202 \\ - 194 \\ \hline \end{array}$

$\begin{array}{r} 880 \\ - 586 \\ \hline \end{array}$

$\begin{array}{r} 420 \\ - 317 \\ \hline \end{array}$

$\begin{array}{r} 610 \\ - 258 \\ \hline \end{array}$

$\begin{array}{r} 950 \\ - 594 \\ \hline \end{array}$

$\begin{array}{r} 190 \\ - 162 \\ \hline \end{array}$

$\begin{array}{r} 840 \\ - 569 \\ \hline \end{array}$

$\begin{array}{r} 503 \\ - 368 \\ \hline \end{array}$

$\begin{array}{r} 301 \\ - 189 \\ \hline \end{array}$

$\begin{array}{r} 805 \\ - 437 \\ \hline \end{array}$

$\begin{array}{r} 170 \\ - 121 \\ \hline \end{array}$

$\begin{array}{r} 530 \\ - 273 \\ \hline \end{array}$

$\begin{array}{r} 760 \\ - 531 \\ \hline \end{array}$

$\begin{array}{r} 600 \\ - 475 \\ \hline \end{array}$

$\begin{array}{r} 704 \\ - 325 \\ \hline \end{array}$

$\begin{array}{r} 700 \\ - 694 \\ \hline \end{array}$

$\begin{array}{r} 900 \\ - 618 \\ \hline \end{array}$

$\begin{array}{r} 407 \\ - 253 \\ \hline \end{array}$

Color Code
0–99 = red
100–199 = blue
200–299 = green
300–399 = yellow

3 digits minus 3 digits with regrouping across zeros

61

Hat Trick

Name _____ Date _____

Subtract.
Show your work.
Write the matching letters from the code.
Read the riddle answer.

What did the hat say to the hat rack?

Code	
18	= A
35	= R
62	= N
107	= H
126	= G
134	= S
171	= D
186	= O
254	= E
375	= L
429	= Y
464	= T
612	= I

390 − 256	850 − 386	407 − 389	700 − 271

___ ___ ___ ___

360 − 253	802 − 548	170 − 135	480 − 226

___ ___ ___ ___ .

740 − 128	530 − 155	906 − 531

305 − 179	900 − 714

___ ___ ___ , ___ ___

603 − 417	208 − 146

510 − 492	901 − 794	703 − 449	602 − 584	500 − 329

___ ___ ___ ___ ___ ___ ___ .

3 digits minus 3 digits with regrouping across zeros

Sylvester's Steps

Name _____   Date _____

Subtract.
Show your work.
Help Sylvester climb up the mountain.
If the answer is even, color the rock brown.

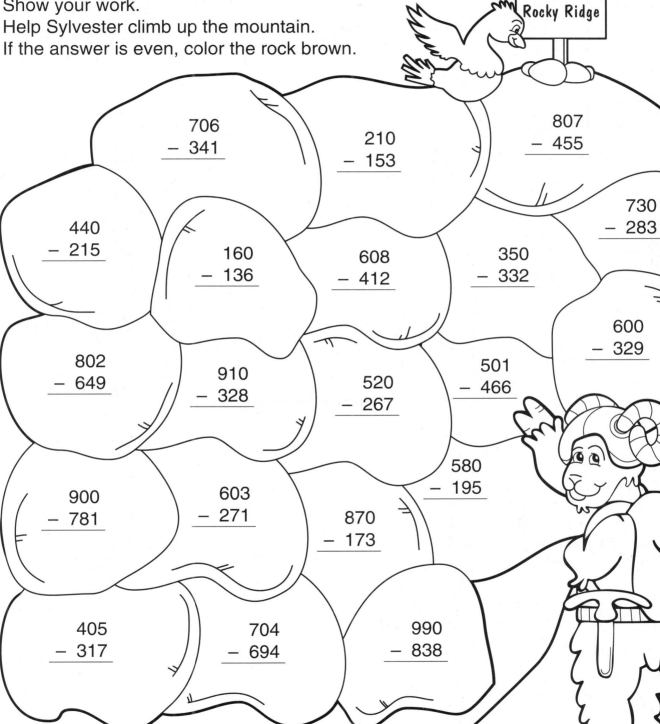

Rocky Ridge

706
− 341

210
− 153

807
− 455

440
− 215

160
− 136

608
− 412

350
− 332

730
− 283

802
− 649

910
− 328

520
− 267

501
− 466

600
− 329

580
− 195

900
− 781

603
− 271

870
− 173

405
− 317

704
− 694

990
− 838

3 digits minus 3 digits with regrouping across zeros

Fairground Follies

Name _____   Date _____

Read.
Solve.
Show your work.

807 guests ride the Ferris wheel. 562 guests ride the bumper cars. How many more guests ride the Ferris wheel than the bumper cars?

_____ guests

709 carousel tickets are sold. 396 guests use their tickets. How many tickets were not used?

_____ tickets

317 visitors see the giant pig before the fair closes. 504 visitors are in line. How many visitors do not see the pig?

_____ visitors

284 butterflies attend the insect show. 380 grasshoppers attend. How many more grasshoppers than butterflies attend?

_____ grasshoppers

402 adults come to the fair. 193 children come to the fair. How many more adults than children come to the fair?

_____ adults

610 candy apples are sold. 452 bags of cotton candy are sold. How many more candy apples are sold?

_____ candy apples

Story problems

Far Out!

Name _____ Date _____

Subtract.
Show your work.
Color by the code.

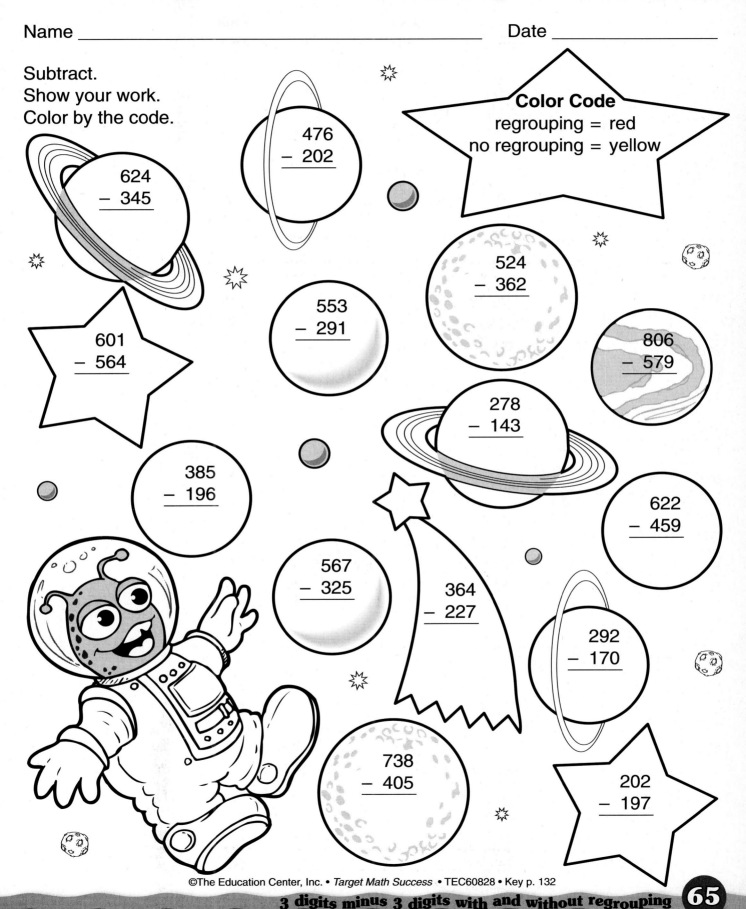

Color Code
regrouping = red
no regrouping = yellow

624
− 345

476
− 202

524
− 362

806
− 579

601
− 564

553
− 291

278
− 143

385
− 196

622
− 459

567
− 325

364
− 227

292
− 170

738
− 405

202
− 197

3 digits minus 3 digits with and without regrouping

Marching Monsters

Name _____   Date _____

Subtract.
Show your work.
Cross off the matching answer.

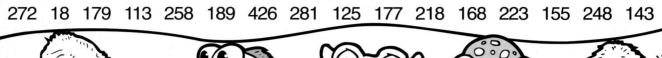

272   18   179   113   258   189   426   281   125   177   218   168   223   155   248   143

468 − 325	625 − 407	461 − 293	264 − 139
387 − 198	402 − 384	942 − 661	259 − 146
423 − 165	597 − 374	677 − 498	905 − 728
807 − 559	753 − 327	523 − 368	829 − 557

Off to the Water Park

Name _____   Date _____

Subtract.
Show your work.

1	5	6	4
−		3	7	7

6	6	1	7
−		2	3	4

3	5	3	8
−		6	2	4

8	6	2	2
−		3	2	3

3	4	5	4
−		8	7	3

7	4	3	7
−		6	8	5

7	2	8	7
−		8	2	5

9	7	4	2
−		6	5	1

4	2	7	6
−		4	3	5

5	8	2	4
−		5	6	9

1	6	5	7
−		4	2	9

8	3	7	5
−		1	2	8

Wiggle
Water Park

4 digits minus 3 digits with one or more regroupings

High-Flying Fun

Name _____ Date _____

Subtract.
Show your work on another sheet of paper.
Color each trapeze that has the correct answer.

| 2,764
− 158
2,606 | 3,621
− 314
3,313 | 1,304
− 533
771 | 6,254
− 735
5,519 | 4,291
− 931
5,222 |

| 5,254
− 321
4,933 | 9,493
− 675
8,828 | 8,932
− 172
8,760 | 5,627
− 155
4,472 | 4,469
− 488
3,987 |

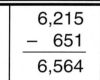

| 6,215
− 651
6,564 | 7,257
− 847
6,410 | 7,429
− 246
7,183 | 2,798
− 459
2,339 | 8,891
− 629
9,520 |

| 3,217
− 766
2,451 | 9,254
− 167
9,387 | 1,731
− 323
1,418 | 3,854
− 289
3,565 | 5,180
− 252
4,928 |

©The Education Center, Inc. • *Target Math Success* • TEC60828 • Key p. 132

4 digits minus 3 digits with one or more regroupings

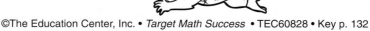

Hop on Over!

Name _____ Date _____

Subtract.
Show your work.
Help the grasshopper get across the stream.
If the answer is **odd,** color the stone **brown.**

6,215
− 187

4,394
− 728

7,510
− 527

3,859
− 465

2,419
− 361

8,746
− 495

1,936
− 457

5,154
− 316

6,457
− 289

2,157
− 596

9,241
− 547

4,473
− 651

7,642
− 872

1,653
− 278

5,372
− 223

8,269
− 833

9,427
− 593

3,288
− 818

4,378
− 795

5,899
− 967

4 digits minus 3 digits with one or more regroupings **69**

Digging Dinosaur

Name _____   Date _____

Subtract.
Show your work.
Cross off the matching answer on the rocks.

1,913 − 127	2,428 − 291	3,535 − 590	4,460 − 909

3,253 − 846	8,740 − 244	9,147 − 913	8,678 − 691	9,189 − 758

1,680 − 790	3,221 − 638	4,832 − 757	1,435 − 547

1,163 − 179	1,254 − 646	8,585 − 467	3,929 − 431

3,440 − 194	9,189 − 361	5,810 − 320

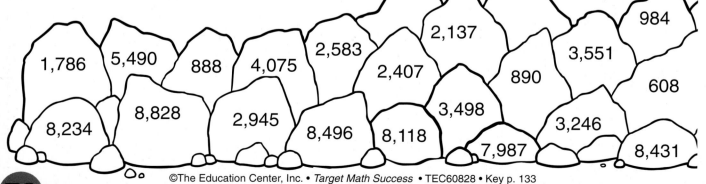

1,786   5,490   888   4,075   2,583   2,137   984
2,407   3,551
890
8,234   8,828   2,945   8,496   8,118   3,498   608
7,987   3,246   8,431

4 digits minus 3 digits with one or more regroupings

Gas Up and Go!

Name _____ Date _____

Read.
Solve.
Show your work.

_____

Rhino's Quick Stop

OPEN

GAS

Rhino sells 1,475 gallons of gas on Saturday. He sells 957 gallons on Sunday. How many more gallons does he sell on Saturday? _____ gallons	Rhino has 1,275 bags of chips. He sells 193. How many bags are left? _____ bags
There are 1,584 candy bars in the store. Rhino sells 176. How many candy bars are left? _____ candy bars	There are 1,439 coffee cups in the store. Rhino sells 557. How many cups are left? _____ cups
There are 1,231 maps in the store. Rhino sells 514. How many maps are left? _____ maps	Rhino has 1,468 drinks for sale. He sells 852. How many drinks are left? _____ drinks

Teamwork

Subtract.
Show your work.

COOKIES

```
  1 9 3 0        5 0 4 0        9 4 7 0        6 0 2 7 2
-   5 3 9      -   4 4 2      -   3 1 5      -     7 6 2
```

```
  2 0 0 6        6 9 0 8        9 0 0 0        5 0 5 0
-   6 5 8      -   7 4 6      -   8 5 3      -   9 8 9
```

```
  3 2 0 0        7 0 5 1        8 0 9 3        4 5 1 0
-   5 6 1      -   4 7 9      -   3 3 8      -   6 9 3
```

```
  4 7 2 0        8 0 0 6        7 0 0 8        3 0 0 0
-   6 8 6      -   7 9 5      -   8 2 1      -   9 1 4
```

4 digits minus 3 digits with regrouping across zeros

One Lucky Find

Name _____   Date _____

Subtract.
Show your work.
Color the coin with the matching answer.

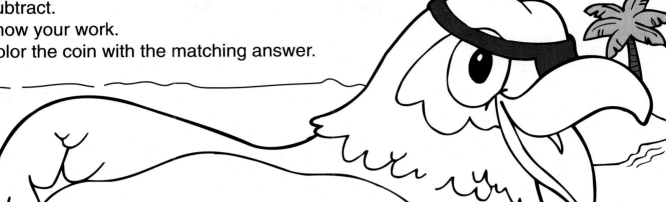

1,084 − 442	5,020 − 341	9,002 − 261	
7,520 − 369	2,040 − 572	6,038 − 153	1,906 − 237
6,010 − 478	3,000 − 983	7,106 − 625	2,007 − 575	5,041 − 785
4,070 − 794	8,500 − 816	3,903 − 692	4,700 − 186

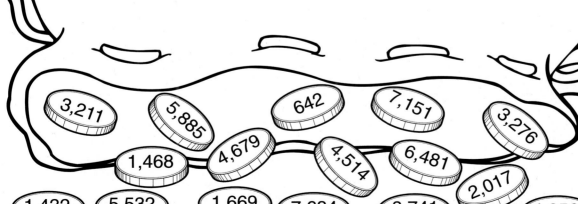

Coins: 3,211 5,885 642 7,151 3,276 1,468 4,679 4,514 6,481 2,017 1,432 5,532 1,669 7,684 8,741 4,256

The Perfect Combination

Name _____   Date _____

Subtract.
Show your work.
Use your answers to complete the puzzles.

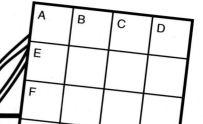

	A	B	C	D
E				
F				
G				

Across

A. 1,900
   − 164

E. 5,800
   − 473

F. 5,007
   − 924

G. 8,103
   − 778

Down

A. 2,000
   − 453

B. 8,081
   − 778

C. 4,005
   − 723

D. 7,019
   − 284

	H	I	J	K
L				
M				
N				

Across

H. 9,300
   − 659

L. 6,000
   − 568

M. 3,018
   − 716

N. 9,870
   − 239

Down

H. 9,460
   − 931

I. 7,032
   − 596

J. 4,470
   − 167

K. 1,506
   − 285

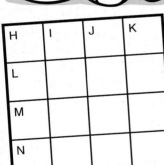

4 digits minus 3 digits with regrouping across zeros

Candid Calculations

Name _____ Date _____

Subtract.
Show your work.

9,280
− 561

7,061
− 765

4,810
− 572

1,094
− 233

6,705
− 389

7,000
− 485

4,030
− 152

3,008
− 837

5,050
− 383

1,509
− 958

2,017
− 746

9,043
− 429

5,100
− 649

8,026
− 914

3,002
− 548

8,300
− 296

6,908
− 654

2,670
− 896

Say Cheese Film

A Busy Place

Name _____ Date _____

Read.
Solve.
Show your work.

Shop and $ave
GROCERY

Betty bakes 3,000 cookies on Monday. She sells 591 cookies. How many cookies are left that night?

_____ cookies

The egg truck delivers 1,705 eggs. 276 eggs are broken. How many eggs are not broken?

_____ eggs

2,100 customers shop at Shop and Save on Wednesday. On Friday, 763 customers shop at the store. How many more customers shop on Wednesday than Friday?

_____ customers

Paulie the produce clerk orders 827 apples. She orders 4,009 oranges. How many more oranges than apples does she order?

_____ oranges

Stockboy Steve places 5,060 cans on the shelves Sunday night. On Monday, he places 934 cans on the shelves. How many more cans are placed on Sunday?

_____ cans

Shop and Save sells 459 boxes of Special Os and 6,308 boxes of Super Crunchers. How many more boxes of Super Crunchers than Special Os are sold?

_____ boxes

Cool Treats

Name _____   Date _____

Subtract.
Show your work.
Use your answers to complete each puzzle.

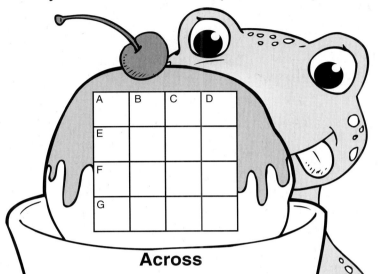

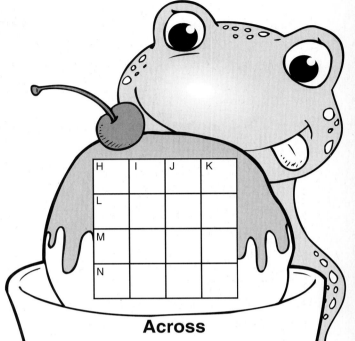

Across

A. 1,682
   − 539

E. 5,966
   − 268

F. 7,201
   − 394

G. 3,795
   − 481

Down

A. 1,984
   − 421

B. 2,265
   − 582

C. 5,837
   − 936

D. 4,021
   − 147

Across

H. 4,310
   − 853

L. 8,832
   − 620

M. 6,424
   − 906

N. 2,058
   − 715

Down

H. 4,514
   − 663

I. 5,108
   − 855

J. 6,089
   − 975

K. 7,390
   − 107

Just Buzzing Around!

Name _____ Date _____

Subtract.
Show your work.
Color the bee with the matching answer.

2,904

7,059 6,418

4,374 7,242 3,621 2,263

8,959 1,937

5,797 5,601 525 4,303

1,306

4,144

8,973

8,231

7,556

4,302 − 158	1,979 − 673	6,830 − 412	8,523 − 967
5,816 − 215	7,461 − 219	3,001 − 738	9,624 − 651	3,783 − 879
6,741 − 944	4,970 − 596	2,258 − 321	8,634 − 403	4,372 − 751
1,057 − 532	9,348 − 389	7,505 − 446	5,197 − 894	

Subtracting Money
Table of Contents

So Hard to Choose!

Name _____ Date _____

Subtract.
Show your work on another sheet of paper.
If the answer is correct, color the car.

New Car Lot
←

$3.22 − .32 $2.90	$1.68 − 1.30 $ .48	
$4.37 − 1.12 $3.25	$3.42 − 1.34 $2.09	$2.96 − 2.63 $ .33
$2.35 − .95 $ .45	$4.72 − 2.51 $2.21	$2.53 − 1.53 $1.50
$3.56 − 1.17 $2.39	$3.16 − 2.15 $1.11	$5.12 − 2.30 $ 2.82
$3.25 − 3.15 $ .10	$4.38 − 1.46 $3.91	$5.50 − 3.50 $2.00

Aha!

Name _____ Date _____

Subtract.
Show your work.
Color by the code.

$7.50
− 5.20

$4.80
− 3.10

$3.80
− 2.70

$1.20
− .90

$4.25
− 3.35

$2.60
− 1.80

$5.20
− 2.30

$3.75
− 3.60

$8.00
− 4.50

$4.95
− 2.00

$7.06
− 4.04

$2.25
− .35

$4.10
− 2.50

$5.50
− 1.70

$5.30
− 2.50

$5.10
− 1.11

Drum Roll, Please!

Name _____ Date _____

Subtract.
Show your work.
Help Danny find his drummer.
Color each box with a difference that is less than $3.50.

$8.60 − 6.28	$4.75 − 2.55	$5.33 − 3.60	$3.50 − .60
$5.10 − .30	$4.62 − .71	$9.32 − 3.76	$9.41 − 4.96	$5.83 − 4.18
$8.15 − 1.13	$5.42 − 3.20	$7.18 − 4.02	$6.46 − 3.23	$9.14 − 5.81
$7.21 − 2.35	$4.15 − .70	$5.40 − 1.35	$8.25 − .75	$5.84 − 1.75
$6.40 − 1.35	$3.85 − 1.22	$6.27 − 2.82		

Batter Up!

Name _____ Date _____

Read.
Solve.
Show your work.

A. Ben has $8.25. He pays $4.00 to watch the baseball game. How much money does Ben have left? _____	B. Tommy has $4.75. A hot dog costs $2.50. He buys one hot dog. How much money does Tommy have left? _____
C. Sarah has $6.00. She buys a bat for $3.50. How much money does Sarah have left? _____	D. Jamie has $12.75. He buys a baseball cap for $7.35. How much money does Jamie have left? _____
E. Abbey has $5.20. A box of popcorn costs $3.50. She buys a box. How much money does Abbey have left? _____	F. Scott has $16.00. He buys a T-shirt for $13.50. How much money does Scott have left? _____

Estimating
Differences

Estimating Differences

Table of Contents

Gone Fishing

Name _____ Date _____

Estimate each difference by rounding to the nearest ten.

$$
\begin{array}{r}
62 \longrightarrow 60 \\
- 18 \longrightarrow -20 \\
\hline
40
\end{array}
$$

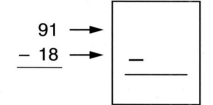

$$
\begin{array}{r}
91 \longrightarrow \\
- 18 \longrightarrow \\
\end{array}
$$

$$
\begin{array}{r}
63 \longrightarrow \\
- 58 \longrightarrow \\
\end{array}
$$

$$
\begin{array}{r}
72 \longrightarrow \\
- 64 \longrightarrow \\
\end{array}
$$

$$
\begin{array}{r}
34 \longrightarrow \\
- 13 \longrightarrow \\
\end{array}
$$

$$
\begin{array}{r}
86 \longrightarrow \\
- 45 \longrightarrow \\
\end{array}
$$

$$
\begin{array}{r}
93 \longrightarrow \\
- 31 \longrightarrow \\
\end{array}
$$

$$
\begin{array}{r}
73 \longrightarrow \\
- 21 \longrightarrow \\
\end{array}
$$

$$
\begin{array}{r}
42 \longrightarrow \\
- 36 \longrightarrow \\
\end{array}
$$

$$
\begin{array}{r}
84 \longrightarrow \\
- 57 \longrightarrow \\
\end{array}
$$

$$
\begin{array}{r}
28 \longrightarrow \\
- 15 \longrightarrow \\
\end{array}
$$

$$
\begin{array}{r}
57 \longrightarrow \\
- 33 \longrightarrow \\
\end{array}
$$

$$
\begin{array}{r}
68 \longrightarrow \\
- 44 \longrightarrow \\
\end{array}
$$

Cock-a-doodle-doo!

Name _____ Date _____

Estimate each difference by rounding to the nearest ten.

$$
\begin{array}{rcr}
47 & \rightarrow & 50 \\
- 31 & \rightarrow & - 30 \\
\hline
& & 20
\end{array}
$$

83 → $\boxed{\ \underline{\quad\quad}\ }$ 52 → $\boxed{\ \underline{\quad\quad}\ }$ 67 → $\boxed{\ \underline{\quad\quad}\ }$
− 49 →

36 →   94 →   64 →
− 29 →   − 51 →   − 43 →

79 →   48 →   85 →
− 22 →   − 14 →   − 56 →

92 →   23 →   71 →
− 37 →   − 19 →   − 62 →

Estimating differences

Sunny Days

Name _____   Date _____

Estimate each difference by rounding to the nearest ten.
Color the petal with the matching answer.

19 − 11	61 − 35	92 − 54
68 − 14	86 − 33	24 − 18
38 − 23	69 − 17	89 − 22
91 − 13	56 − 27	83 − 46
42 − 34	77 − 39	94 − 42
53 − 48		

Petals: 30 20 0 60 40 10 50 10 40 30 0 80 70 20 60 50

Downhill Divas

Name _____ Date _____

Estimate each difference by rounding to the nearest hundred.

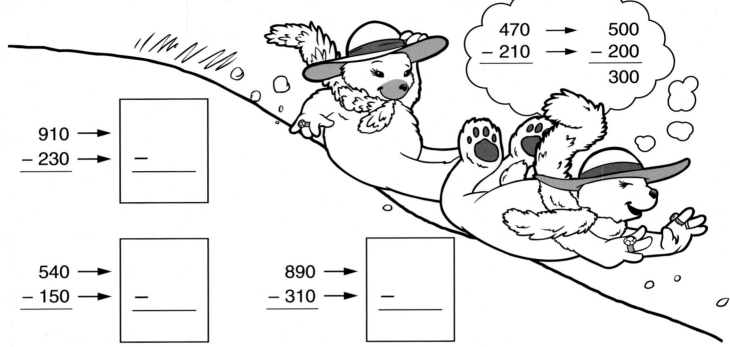

$$
\begin{array}{r}
470 \rightarrow 500 \\
-\,210 \rightarrow -\,200 \\
\hline
300
\end{array}
$$

910 →
− 230 → ___ − ___

540 →
− 150 → ___ − ___

890 →
− 310 → ___ − ___

170 →
− 110 → ___ − ___

740 →
− 510 → ___ − ___

680 →
− 320 → ___ − ___

850 →
− 720 → ___ − ___

330 →
− 260 → ___ − ___

280 →
− 120 → ___ − ___

460 →
− 240 → ___ − ___

670 →
− 380 → ___ − ___

570 →
− 160 → ___ − ___

Time to Celebrate

Name _____   Date _____

Estimate each difference by rounding to the nearest hundred.

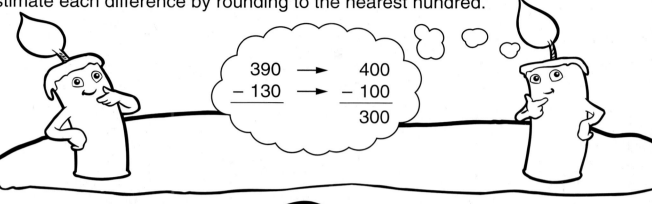

$$\begin{array}{rcr} 390 & \rightarrow & 400 \\ -130 & \rightarrow & -100 \\ \hline & & 300 \end{array}$$

$$\begin{array}{rcl} 380 & \rightarrow & \underline{} \\ -250 & \rightarrow & -\underline{} \\ \hline \end{array}$$

$$\begin{array}{rcl} 820 & \rightarrow & \underline{} \\ -710 & \rightarrow & -\underline{} \\ \hline \end{array}$$

$$\begin{array}{rcl} 550 & \rightarrow & \underline{} \\ -120 & \rightarrow & -\underline{} \\ \hline \end{array}$$

$$\begin{array}{rcl} 260 & \rightarrow & \underline{} \\ -110 & \rightarrow & -\underline{} \\ \hline \end{array}$$

$$\begin{array}{rcl} 930 & \rightarrow & \underline{} \\ -450 & \rightarrow & -\underline{} \\ \hline \end{array}$$

$$\begin{array}{rcl} 420 & \rightarrow & \underline{} \\ -370 & \rightarrow & -\underline{} \\ \hline \end{array}$$

$$\begin{array}{rcl} 590 & \rightarrow & \underline{} \\ -330 & \rightarrow & -\underline{} \\ \hline \end{array}$$

$$\begin{array}{rcl} 610 & \rightarrow & \underline{} \\ -350 & \rightarrow & -\underline{} \\ \hline \end{array}$$

$$\begin{array}{rcl} 940 & \rightarrow & \underline{} \\ -210 & \rightarrow & -\underline{} \\ \hline \end{array}$$

$$\begin{array}{rcl} 780 & \rightarrow & \underline{} \\ -570 & \rightarrow & -\underline{} \\ \hline \end{array}$$

$$\begin{array}{rcl} 690 & \rightarrow & \underline{} \\ -430 & \rightarrow & -\underline{} \\ \hline \end{array}$$

$$\begin{array}{rcl} 770 & \rightarrow & \underline{} \\ -630 & \rightarrow & -\underline{} \\ \hline \end{array}$$

Coconuts in Paradise

Name _____   Date _____

Estimate each difference by rounding to the nearest hundred.
Cross off the matching answer on the palm tree.

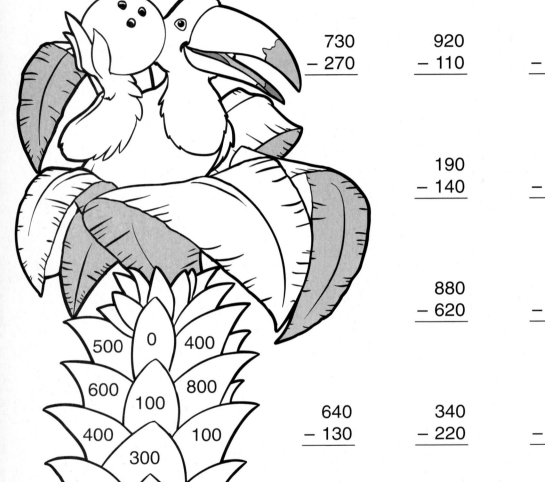

$$730 - 270$$ $$920 - 110$$ $$370 - 320$$ $$660 - 510$$

$$190 - 140$$ $$580 - 250$$ $$930 - 440$$

$$880 - 620$$ $$290 - 180$$ $$750 - 230$$

$$640 - 130$$ $$340 - 220$$ $$840 - 380$$ $$410 - 390$$

$$860 - 540$$ $$530 - 310$$ $$470 - 210$$ $$520 - 480$$

 Estimating differences

Choose the Correct Operation

Table of Contents

Proud Button Collectors

Name _____ Date _____

Read.
Solve.
Show your work.

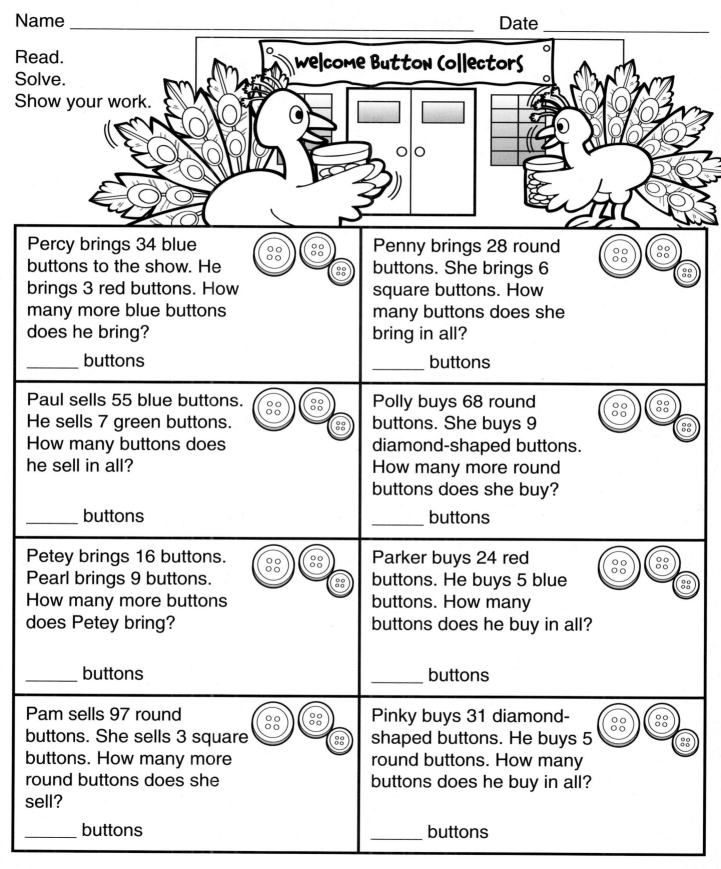

Welcome Button Collectors

Percy brings 34 blue buttons to the show. He brings 3 red buttons. How many more blue buttons does he bring?

_____ buttons

Penny brings 28 round buttons. She brings 6 square buttons. How many buttons does she bring in all?

_____ buttons

Paul sells 55 blue buttons. He sells 7 green buttons. How many buttons does he sell in all?

_____ buttons

Polly buys 68 round buttons. She buys 9 diamond-shaped buttons. How many more round buttons does she buy?

_____ buttons

Petey brings 16 buttons. Pearl brings 9 buttons. How many more buttons does Petey bring?

_____ buttons

Parker buys 24 red buttons. He buys 5 blue buttons. How many buttons does he buy in all?

_____ buttons

Pam sells 97 round buttons. She sells 3 square buttons. How many more round buttons does she sell?

_____ buttons

Pinky buys 31 diamond-shaped buttons. He buys 5 round buttons. How many buttons does he buy in all?

_____ buttons

A Day at the Doughnut Shop

Name _____ Date _____

Read.
Solve.
Show your work.

Wally sells 26 glazed doughnuts. He sells 18 chocolate doughnuts. How many doughnuts does he sell in all?

_____ doughnuts

Wally makes 24 jelly doughnuts. He makes 12 cake doughnuts. How many more jelly doughnuts does he make?

_____ doughnuts

Wally sells 64 blueberry doughnuts. He sells 27 lemon doughnuts. How many more blueberry doughnuts does he sell?

_____ doughnuts

Perry Parrot buys 25 chocolate doughnuts. She buys 32 glazed doughnuts. How many doughnuts does she buy in all?

_____ doughnuts

Jenny Jay buys 78 lemon doughnuts. She buys 44 blueberry doughnuts. How many more lemon doughnuts does she buy?

_____ doughnuts

Calvin Crow buys 14 cake doughnuts. He buys 33 jelly doughnuts. How many doughnuts does he buy in all?

_____ doughnuts

How Does Your Garden Grow?

Name _____   Date _____

Read.
Solve.
Show your work.

Rudy plants 372 sunflowers.
He plants 141 petunias.
How many more
sunflowers does he
plant?

_____ sunflowers

Shelly plants 218 daffodils.
She plants 346 tulips.
How many flowers does
she plant in all?

_____ flowers

Rudy plants 512 pumpkins.
He plants 207 carrots. How
many more pumpkins does
he plant?

_____ pumpkins

Shelly plants 433 string
beans. She plants 325 lima
beans. How many beans
does she plant in all?

_____ beans

Rudy picks 337 red roses.
He picks 165 yellow
roses. How many more
red roses does he pick?

_____ roses

Shelly harvests 546 sweet
potatoes. She harvests
243 white potatoes. How
many potatoes does she
harvest in all?

_____ potatoes

Hit the Road!

Name _____   Date _____

Read.
Solve.
Show your work.

Gator Brothers
Swamp City or Bust!

During the first week of January, the Gator Brothers drive 1,208 miles. During the second week, they drive 1,351 miles. How many miles do they drive in all? _____ miles	In February, the brothers drive 4,640 miles. In March they drive 2,317 miles. How many more miles do they drive in February? _____ miles
During the third week of April, the brothers drive 2,572 miles. During the fourth week of April, they drive 1,340 miles. How many miles do they drive in all? _____ miles	In May, the brothers drive 3,611 miles. In June, they drive 2,201 miles. How many more miles do they drive in May? _____ miles
During the busy season, the brothers drive 3,222 miles in one week. During the next week, they drive 4,623 miles. How many miles do they drive in all? _____ miles	During their longest trip, the brothers drive 6,483 miles. During their shortest trip, they drive 1,168 miles. How many more miles do they drive on their longest trip? _____ miles

Parent Communication and Student Checkups

Table of Contents

How to Administer the Checkups

Both checkups can be given at the same time, or Checkup B can be given as a follow-up test for students who did not do well on Checkup A. The checkups will help you determine which students have mastered a skill and which students may need more practice.

Show-Your-Work Grids

For students who need help aligning numbers properly when writing vertical subtraction problems, check out the show-your-work grids on pages 122–123.

Student Progress Chart

_____ (student)		Date	Number Correct	Comments
Checkup 1: 2 digits minus 1 digit without regrouping	A			
	B			
Checkup 2: 2 digits minus 1 digit with regrouping	A			
	B			
Checkup 3: 2 digits minus 2 digits without regrouping	A			
	B			
Checkup 4: 2 digits minus 2 digits with regrouping	A			
	B			
Checkup 5: 3 digits minus 2 digits without regrouping	A			
	B			
Checkup 6: 3 digits minus 2 digits with regrouping	A			
	B			
Checkup 7: 3 digits minus 3 digits with regrouping	A			
	B			
Checkup 8: 3 digits minus 3 digits with regrouping across zeros	A			
	B			
Checkup 9: 4 digits minus 3 digits with regrouping	A			
	B			
Checkup 10: 4 digits minus 3 digits with regrouping across zeros	A			
	B			

It's Time to Take Aim!

On _____ our class will be having a checkup on subtraction of larger numbers. To help your child prepare, please spend about 20 minutes reviewing math problems that involve **subtracting 1 digit from 2 digits without regrouping.** Thanks for your help!

Subtraction Refresher

Guide your child through the first problem at the right using the steps listed below. Next, have him complete the second problem independently, verbalizing each step as he solves the problem. Then have him complete the remaining problems on his own.

Step 1
Do: Point out the numbers in the ones column.
Ask: Do I need to regroup?
(No.)

T	O
4	7
−	4

Step 2
Do: Subtract the numbers in the ones column.

T	O
4	7
−	4
	3

Step 3
Do: Bring the number from the tens column down to the answer.

T	O
4	7
−	4
4	3

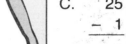

Try using these steps!

Target These!

A. $\begin{array}{r} 47 \\ -\ 4 \\ \hline \end{array}$ B. $\begin{array}{r} 89 \\ -\ 6 \\ \hline \end{array}$

C. $\begin{array}{r} 25 \\ -\ 1 \\ \hline \end{array}$ D. $\begin{array}{r} 73 \\ -\ 2 \\ \hline \end{array}$

E. $\begin{array}{r} 56 \\ -\ 3 \\ \hline \end{array}$ F. $\begin{array}{r} 38 \\ -\ 5 \\ \hline \end{array}$

G. $\begin{array}{r} 14 \\ -\ 2 \\ \hline \end{array}$

H. $\begin{array}{r} 69 \\ -\ 4 \\ \hline \end{array}$

Answers: 43, 83, 24, 71, 53, 33, 12, 65

If your child is quick to solve the remaining math problems correctly, an occasional review may be all he needs. But if several of the answers are incorrect, it's a good idea to spend some time each day having your child work through a problem or two at home until he's mastered this skill.

Checkup 1

Name _____

Date _____

A.
$$\begin{array}{r} 14 \\ -\ 2 \\ \hline \end{array}$$
$$\begin{array}{r} 85 \\ -\ 2 \\ \hline \end{array}$$
$$\begin{array}{r} 51 \\ -\ 0 \\ \hline \end{array}$$
$$\begin{array}{r} 34 \\ -\ 3 \\ \hline \end{array}$$
$$\begin{array}{r} 62 \\ -\ 1 \\ \hline \end{array}$$

B.
$$\begin{array}{r} 59 \\ -\ 1 \\ \hline \end{array}$$
$$\begin{array}{r} 74 \\ -\ 2 \\ \hline \end{array}$$
$$\begin{array}{r} 37 \\ -\ 5 \\ \hline \end{array}$$
$$\begin{array}{r} 17 \\ -\ 2 \\ \hline \end{array}$$
$$\begin{array}{r} 46 \\ -\ 3 \\ \hline \end{array}$$

C.
$$\begin{array}{r} 62 \\ -\ 2 \\ \hline \end{array}$$
$$\begin{array}{r} 23 \\ -\ 1 \\ \hline \end{array}$$
$$\begin{array}{r} 71 \\ -\ 0 \\ \hline \end{array}$$
$$\begin{array}{r} 44 \\ -\ 1 \\ \hline \end{array}$$
$$\begin{array}{r} 83 \\ -\ 2 \\ \hline \end{array}$$

D.
$$\begin{array}{r} 95 \\ -\ 4 \\ \hline \end{array}$$
$$\begin{array}{r} 26 \\ -\ 2 \\ \hline \end{array}$$
$$\begin{array}{r} 68 \\ -\ 6 \\ \hline \end{array}$$
$$\begin{array}{r} 47 \\ -\ 3 \\ \hline \end{array}$$
$$\begin{array}{r} 29 \\ -\ 7 \\ \hline \end{array}$$

E.
$$\begin{array}{r} 83 \\ -\ 0 \\ \hline \end{array}$$
$$\begin{array}{r} 56 \\ -\ 4 \\ \hline \end{array}$$
$$\begin{array}{r} 35 \\ -\ 3 \\ \hline \end{array}$$
$$\begin{array}{r} 69 \\ -\ 8 \\ \hline \end{array}$$
$$\begin{array}{r} 98 \\ -\ 5 \\ \hline \end{array}$$

Test A: 2 digits minus 1 digit without regrouping

Checkup 1

Name _____

Date _____

A.
$$\begin{array}{r} 42 \\ -\ 1 \\ \hline \end{array}$$
$$\begin{array}{r} 23 \\ -\ 2 \\ \hline \end{array}$$
$$\begin{array}{r} 52 \\ -\ 0 \\ \hline \end{array}$$
$$\begin{array}{r} 18 \\ -\ 4 \\ \hline \end{array}$$
$$\begin{array}{r} 65 \\ -\ 3 \\ \hline \end{array}$$

B.
$$\begin{array}{r} 26 \\ -\ 3 \\ \hline \end{array}$$
$$\begin{array}{r} 69 \\ -\ 5 \\ \hline \end{array}$$
$$\begin{array}{r} 14 \\ -\ 1 \\ \hline \end{array}$$
$$\begin{array}{r} 31 \\ -\ 0 \\ \hline \end{array}$$
$$\begin{array}{r} 97 \\ -\ 4 \\ \hline \end{array}$$

C.
$$\begin{array}{r} 57 \\ -\ 5 \\ \hline \end{array}$$
$$\begin{array}{r} 72 \\ -\ 1 \\ \hline \end{array}$$
$$\begin{array}{r} 35 \\ -\ 2 \\ \hline \end{array}$$
$$\begin{array}{r} 46 \\ -\ 3 \\ \hline \end{array}$$
$$\begin{array}{r} 84 \\ -\ 1 \\ \hline \end{array}$$

D.
$$\begin{array}{r} 86 \\ -\ 2 \\ \hline \end{array}$$
$$\begin{array}{r} 38 \\ -\ 4 \\ \hline \end{array}$$
$$\begin{array}{r} 45 \\ -\ 3 \\ \hline \end{array}$$
$$\begin{array}{r} 23 \\ -\ 2 \\ \hline \end{array}$$
$$\begin{array}{r} 77 \\ -\ 3 \\ \hline \end{array}$$

E.
$$\begin{array}{r} 19 \\ -\ 6 \\ \hline \end{array}$$
$$\begin{array}{r} 67 \\ -\ 2 \\ \hline \end{array}$$
$$\begin{array}{r} 93 \\ -\ 1 \\ \hline \end{array}$$
$$\begin{array}{r} 58 \\ -\ 3 \\ \hline \end{array}$$
$$\begin{array}{r} 84 \\ -\ 3 \\ \hline \end{array}$$

Test B: 2 digits minus 1 digit without regrouping

It's Time to Take Aim!

On _____ our class will be having a checkup on subtraction of larger numbers. To help your child prepare, please spend about 20 minutes reviewing math problems that involve **subtracting 1 digit from 2 digits with regrouping.** Thanks for your help!

Subtraction Refresher

Guide your child through the first problem at the right using the steps listed below. Next, have him complete the second problem independently, verbalizing each step as he solves the problem. Then have him complete the remaining problems on his own.

Step 1
Do: Point out the numbers in the ones column.
Ask: Do I need to regroup?
(Yes.)

T	O
4	2
−	8

Step 2
Do: Borrow from the tens column.

T	O
3	12
4̸	2̸
−	8

Step 3
Do: Subtract the numbers in the ones column.

T	O
3	12
4̸	2̸
−	8
	4

Step 4
Do: Bring the number from the tens column down to the answer.

T	O
3	12
4̸	2̸
−	8
3	4

Try using these steps!

Target These!

A.
```
  42
−  8
```

B.
```
  84
−  6
```

C.
```
  61
−  7
```

D.
```
  94
−  8
```

E.
```
  43
−  5
```

F.
```
  25
−  9
```

G.
```
  58
−  9
```

H.
```
  76
−  7
```

Answers: 34, 78, 54, 86, 38, 16, 49, 69

Checkup 2

Name _____

Date _____

A. $\begin{array}{r} 85 \\ -\ 6 \\ \hline \end{array}$ $\begin{array}{r} 52 \\ -\ 4 \\ \hline \end{array}$ $\begin{array}{r} 24 \\ -\ 7 \\ \hline \end{array}$ $\begin{array}{r} 64 \\ -\ 5 \\ \hline \end{array}$ $\begin{array}{r} 35 \\ -\ 7 \\ \hline \end{array}$

B. $\begin{array}{r} 46 \\ -\ 9 \\ \hline \end{array}$ $\begin{array}{r} 11 \\ -\ 8 \\ \hline \end{array}$ $\begin{array}{r} 52 \\ -\ 6 \\ \hline \end{array}$ $\begin{array}{r} 26 \\ -\ 7 \\ \hline \end{array}$ $\begin{array}{r} 97 \\ -\ 8 \\ \hline \end{array}$

C. $\begin{array}{r} 74 \\ -\ 9 \\ \hline \end{array}$ $\begin{array}{r} 83 \\ -\ 5 \\ \hline \end{array}$ $\begin{array}{r} 98 \\ -\ 9 \\ \hline \end{array}$ $\begin{array}{r} 62 \\ -\ 7 \\ \hline \end{array}$ $\begin{array}{r} 25 \\ -\ 9 \\ \hline \end{array}$

D. $\begin{array}{r} 72 \\ -\ 6 \\ \hline \end{array}$ $\begin{array}{r} 45 \\ -\ 8 \\ \hline \end{array}$ $\begin{array}{r} 34 \\ -\ 5 \\ \hline \end{array}$ $\begin{array}{r} 83 \\ -\ 8 \\ \hline \end{array}$ $\begin{array}{r} 54 \\ -\ 6 \\ \hline \end{array}$

E. $\begin{array}{r} 62 \\ -\ 8 \\ \hline \end{array}$ $\begin{array}{r} 33 \\ -\ 6 \\ \hline \end{array}$ $\begin{array}{r} 77 \\ -\ 9 \\ \hline \end{array}$ $\begin{array}{r} 95 \\ -\ 7 \\ \hline \end{array}$ $\begin{array}{r} 16 \\ -\ 8 \\ \hline \end{array}$

Test A: 2 digits minus 1 digit with regrouping

Checkup 2

Name _____

Date _____

A. $\begin{array}{r} 26 \\ -\ 7 \\ \hline \end{array}$ $\begin{array}{r} 13 \\ -\ 4 \\ \hline \end{array}$ $\begin{array}{r} 85 \\ -\ 8 \\ \hline \end{array}$ $\begin{array}{r} 44 \\ -\ 7 \\ \hline \end{array}$ $\begin{array}{r} 62 \\ -\ 5 \\ \hline \end{array}$

B. $\begin{array}{r} 91 \\ -\ 4 \\ \hline \end{array}$ $\begin{array}{r} 78 \\ -\ 9 \\ \hline \end{array}$ $\begin{array}{r} 52 \\ -\ 8 \\ \hline \end{array}$ $\begin{array}{r} 36 \\ -\ 9 \\ \hline \end{array}$ $\begin{array}{r} 73 \\ -\ 6 \\ \hline \end{array}$

C. $\begin{array}{r} 45 \\ -\ 9 \\ \hline \end{array}$ $\begin{array}{r} 22 \\ -\ 6 \\ \hline \end{array}$ $\begin{array}{r} 84 \\ -\ 5 \\ \hline \end{array}$ $\begin{array}{r} 71 \\ -\ 3 \\ \hline \end{array}$ $\begin{array}{r} 97 \\ -\ 8 \\ \hline \end{array}$

D. $\begin{array}{r} 56 \\ -\ 8 \\ \hline \end{array}$ $\begin{array}{r} 94 \\ -\ 9 \\ \hline \end{array}$ $\begin{array}{r} 33 \\ -\ 5 \\ \hline \end{array}$ $\begin{array}{r} 65 \\ -\ 7 \\ \hline \end{array}$ $\begin{array}{r} 42 \\ -\ 7 \\ \hline \end{array}$

E. $\begin{array}{r} 33 \\ -\ 8 \\ \hline \end{array}$ $\begin{array}{r} 65 \\ -\ 6 \\ \hline \end{array}$ $\begin{array}{r} 81 \\ -\ 5 \\ \hline \end{array}$ $\begin{array}{r} 57 \\ -\ 9 \\ \hline \end{array}$ $\begin{array}{r} 24 \\ -\ 6 \\ \hline \end{array}$

Test B: 2 digits minus 1 digit with regrouping

It's Time to Take Aim!

On _____ our class will be having a checkup on subtraction of larger numbers. To help your child prepare, please spend about 20 minutes reviewing math problems that involve **subtracting 2 digits from 2 digits without regrouping.** Thanks for your help!

Subtraction Refresher

Guide your child through the first problem at the right using the steps listed below. Next, have him complete the second problem independently, verbalizing each step as he solves the problem. Then have him complete the remaining problems on his own.

Step 1
Do: Point out the numbers in the ones column.
Ask: Do I need to regroup? *(No.)*

T	O
3	2
− 1	1

Step 2
Do: Subtract the numbers in the ones column.

T	O
3	2
− 1	1
	1

Step 3
Do: Subtract the numbers in the tens column.

T	O
3	2
− 1	1
2	1

Try using these steps!

Target These!

A.
```
  32
− 11
```

B.
```
  64
− 32
```

C.
```
  89
− 23
```

D.
```
  25
− 12
```

E.
```
  46
− 34
```

F.
```
  78
− 55
```

G.
```
  97
− 32
```

H.
```
  53
− 41
```

Answers: 21, 32, 66, 13, 12, 23, 65, 12

If your child is quick to solve the remaining math problems correctly, an occasional review may be all he needs. But if several of the answers are incorrect, it's a good idea to spend some time each day having your child work through a problem or two at home until he's mastered this skill.

Checkup 3

Name _____ Date _____

Test A: 2 digits minus 2 digits without regrouping

A. 56 − 44	39 − 12	75 − 23	68 − 54	82 − 30
B. 57 − 23	83 − 51	26 − 12	47 − 24	74 − 43
C. 95 − 74	78 − 63	27 − 26	32 − 11	68 − 56
D. 44 − 13	63 − 52	97 − 42	89 − 25	46 − 13
E. 39 − 23	57 − 25	96 − 61	74 − 72	58 − 36

Checkup 3

Name _____ Date _____

A. 68 − 56	54 − 32	29 − 15	56 − 43	82 − 61
B. 79 − 34	18 − 17	39 − 27	93 − 51	44 − 13
C. 35 − 14	58 − 25	91 − 30	46 − 22	73 − 23
D. 63 − 42	29 − 12	57 − 15	34 − 21	89 − 36
E. 74 − 41	93 − 41	42 − 20	67 − 41	85 − 43

Test B: 2 digits minus 2 digits without regrouping

It's Time to Take Aim!

On _____ our class will be having a checkup on subtraction of larger numbers. To help your child prepare, please spend about 20 minutes reviewing math problems that involve **subtracting 2 digits from 2 digits with regrouping.** Thanks for your help!

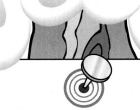

Target These!

A.	42	B	74
	− 18		− 37

C.	57	D.	25
	− 28		− 17

E.	41	F.	82
	− 37		− 24

G.	36
	− 19

H.	63
	− 48

Subtraction Refresher

Guide your child through the first problem at the right using the steps listed below. Next, have him complete the second problem independently, verbalizing each step as he solves the problem. Then have him complete the remaining problems on his own.

Step 1
Do: Point out the numbers in the ones column.
Ask: Do I need to regroup?
(Yes.)

T	O
4	2
− 1	8

Step 2
Do: Borrow from the tens column.

T	O
3	12
~~4~~	~~2~~
− 1	8

Step 3
Do: Subtract the numbers in the ones column.

T	O
3	12
~~4~~	~~2~~
− 1	8
	4

Try using these steps!

Step 4
Do: Subtract the numbers in the tens column.

T	O
3	12
~~4~~	~~2~~
− 1	8
2	4

Answers: 24, 37, 29, 8, 4, 58, 17, 15

If your child is quick to solve the remaining math problems correctly, an occasional review may be all he needs. But if several of the answers are incorrect, it's a good idea to spend some time each day having your child work through a problem or two at home until he's mastered this skill.

Checkup 4

Name _____   Date _____

A.	51 − 14	72 − 39	44 − 15	63 − 58
B.	86 − 57	64 − 29	51 − 27	37 − 18
C.	85 − 47	43 − 25	64 − 38	92 − 67
D.	58 − 39	64 − 17	72 − 28	73 − 46
E.	91 − 45	83 − 37	27 − 19	95 − 38

Test A: 2 digits minus 2 digits with regrouping

Checkup 4

Name _____   Date _____

A.	74 − 65	63 − 27	51 − 25	32 − 13
B.	58 − 49	41 − 19	84 − 67	86 − 39
C.	63 − 46	25 − 19	74 − 48	51 − 28
D.	93 − 74	82 − 15	36 − 28	63 − 34
E.	71 − 46	97 − 28	44 − 19	52 − 34

Test B: 2 digits minus 2 digits with regrouping

It's Time to Take Aim!

On _____ our class will be having a checkup on subtraction of larger numbers. To help your child prepare, please spend about 20 minutes reviewing math problems that involve **subtracting 2 digits from 3 digits without regrouping.** Thanks for your help!

Subtraction Refresher

Step 1
Have your child complete the problem below. During a recent checkup, your child showed an understanding of this type of subtraction. Confirm that his answer is correct.

$$
\begin{array}{r}
84 \\
- 21 \\
\hline
\end{array}
$$

Step 2
Have your child complete problem A at the right. This problem requires an additional step. (This step is outlined below.) Confirm that your child's answer is correct.

Additional step:
Bring down the number in the hundreds column.

H	T	O
6	9	3
−	5	2
6	4	1

Step 3
Have your child complete the remaining practice problems on his own.

Try using these steps!

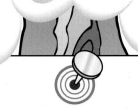

Target These!

A.	693 − 52	B.	486 − 43
C.	847 − 25	D.	175 − 43
E.	765 − 41	F.	929 − 17
		G.	247 − 32
		H.	568 − 56

Step 1 answer: 63

If your child is quick to solve the remaining math problems correctly, an occasional review may be all he needs. But if several of the answers are incorrect, it's a good idea to spend some time each day having your child work through a problem or two at home until he's mastered this skill.

Checkup 5

Name _____ Date _____

A.	563 − 21	979 − 26	665 − 42	287 − 71	195 − 24
B.	714 − 12	695 − 43	368 − 31	447 − 16	269 − 21
C.	486 − 55	778 − 32	196 − 84	958 − 13	479 − 45
D.	567 − 15	258 − 32	379 − 47	826 − 14	987 − 62
E.	688 − 38	394 − 33	565 − 14	238 − 24	869 − 35

Test A: 3 digits minus 2 digits without regrouping

111

Checkup 5

Name _____ Date _____

A.	363 − 53	195 − 11	978 − 17	626 − 16	889 − 33
B.	485 − 15	394 − 72	879 − 55	169 − 12	563 − 41
C.	178 − 67	782 − 21	949 − 28	645 − 34	427 − 20
D.	479 − 24	637 − 23	284 − 41	896 − 63	568 − 45
E.	594 − 50	765 − 22	149 − 13	368 − 36	732 − 20

Test B: 3 digits minus 2 digits without regrouping

It's Time to Take Aim!

On _____ our class will be having a checkup on subtraction of larger numbers. To help your child prepare, please spend about 20 minutes reviewing math problems that involve **subtracting 2 digits from 3 digits with regrouping.** Thanks for your help!

Subtraction Refresher

Step 1
Have your child complete the problem below. During a recent checkup, your child showed an understanding of this type of subtraction. Confirm that his answer is correct.

$$\begin{array}{r} 76 \\ -\ 48 \\ \hline \end{array}$$

Step 2
Have your child complete problem A at the right. This problem requires two additional steps. (These steps are outlined below.) Confirm that your child's answer is correct.

Additional Steps
1. When the tens column cannot be subtracted, borrow from the hundreds column.
2. Bring the number from the hundreds column down to the answer.

H	T	O
²$\cancel{3}$	¹³$\cancel{4}$	³¹³$\cancel{3}$
−	5	5
2	8	8

Step 3
Have your child complete the remaining practice problems on his own.

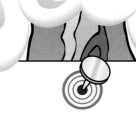

Target These!

A.
$$\begin{array}{r} 343 \\ -\ 55 \\ \hline \end{array}$$

B.
$$\begin{array}{r} 328 \\ -\ 79 \\ \hline \end{array}$$

C.
$$\begin{array}{r} 971 \\ -\ 65 \\ \hline \end{array}$$

D.
$$\begin{array}{r} 143 \\ -\ 81 \\ \hline \end{array}$$

E.
$$\begin{array}{r} 815 \\ -\ 68 \\ \hline \end{array}$$

F.
$$\begin{array}{r} 528 \\ -\ 79 \\ \hline \end{array}$$

G.
$$\begin{array}{r} 236 \\ -\ 27 \\ \hline \end{array}$$

H.
$$\begin{array}{r} 725 \\ -\ 43 \\ \hline \end{array}$$

Try using these steps!

If your child is quick to solve the remaining math problems correctly, an occasional review may be all he needs. But if several of the answers are incorrect, it's a good idea to spend some time each day having your child work through a problem or two at home until he's mastered this skill.

Checkup 6

Name _____

Date _____

A.
448	725	373	125	516
− 39	− 37	− 45	− 86	− 73

B.
953	458	124	634	259
− 62	− 96	− 72	− 85	− 82

C.
313	576	892	657	121
− 67	− 89	− 67	− 85	− 54

D.
489	253	375	852	942
− 91	− 78	− 68	− 46	− 89

E.
653	792	936	532	284
− 94	− 46	− 82	− 61	− 36

Test A: 3 digits minus 2 digits with regrouping

©The Education Center, Inc. • *Target Math Success* • TEC60828 • Key p. 136

Checkup 6

Name _____

Date _____

A.
112	595	853	483	971
− 86	− 77	− 37	− 45	− 37

B.
328	835	627	385	739
− 81	− 69	− 42	− 96	− 93

C.
226	732	584	916	491
− 49	− 75	− 29	− 54	− 52

D.
973	639	251	757	524
− 96	− 48	− 26	− 85	− 76

E.
372	636	412	125	847
− 19	− 57	− 58	− 39	− 78

Test B: 3 digits minus 2 digits with regrouping

©The Education Center, Inc. • *Target Math Success* • TEC60828 • Key p. 136

113

It's Time to Take Aim!

On _____ our class will be having a checkup on subtraction of larger numbers. To help your child prepare, please spend about 20 minutes reviewing math problems that involve **subtracting 3 digits from 3 digits with regrouping.** Thanks for your help!

Subtraction Refresher

Step 1
Have your child complete the problem below. During a recent checkup, your child showed an understanding of this type of subtraction. Confirm that his answer is correct.

$$\begin{array}{r} 723 \\ -\ 45 \\ \hline \end{array}$$

Step 2
Have your child complete problem A at the right. This problem requires an additional step. (This step is outlined below.) Confirm that your child's answer is correct.

Additional Step
1. Subtract the numbers in the hundreds column.

H	T	O
²3̶	¹³4̶	³3̶¹³
− 1	6	8
1	7	5

Step 3
Have your child complete the remaining practice problems on his own.

Target These!

A.	343 − 168	B.	567 − 248
C.	918 − 139	D.	739 − 364
E.	285 − 119	F.	832 − 378
G.	574 − 482		
		H.	614 − 258

Try using these steps!

If your child is quick to solve the remaining math problems correctly, an occasional review may be all he needs. But if several of the answers are incorrect, it's a good idea to spend some time each day having your child work through a problem or two at home until he's mastered this skill.

Checkup 7

Name _____ Date _____

A.	776 − 382	531 − 269	782 − 564	948 − 689	814 − 265
B.	457 − 271	852 − 487	637 − 578	315 − 289	667 − 282
C.	541 − 362	262 − 133	931 − 497	782 − 691	465 − 197
D.	849 − 685	643 − 498	471 − 394	523 − 484	844 − 537
E.	362 − 179	913 − 232	758 − 449	247 − 158	951 − 399

Test A: 3 digits minus 3 digits with regrouping

©The Education Center, Inc. • *Target Math Success* • TEC60828 • Key p. 136

Checkup 7

Name _____ Date _____

A.	752 − 427	838 − 659	655 − 278	544 − 393	717 − 169
B.	933 − 714	749 − 274	273 − 187	662 − 395	461 − 353
C.	381 − 158	537 − 259	628 − 469	895 − 356	925 − 686
D.	537 − 488	667 − 276	791 − 349	342 − 259	813 − 426
E.	412 − 257	825 − 718	554 − 146	962 − 584	418 − 144

Test B: 3 digits minus 3 digits with regrouping

©The Education Center, Inc. • *Target Math Success* • TEC60828 • Key p. 136

It's Time to Take Aim!

On _____ our class will be having a checkup on subtraction of larger numbers. To help your child prepare, please spend about 20 minutes reviewing math problems that involve **subtracting 3 digits from 3 digits with regrouping across zeros.** Thanks for your help!

Subtraction Refresher

Step 1
Have your child complete the problem below. During a recent checkup, your child showed an understanding of this type of subtraction. Confirm that his answer is correct.

$$\begin{array}{r} 823 \\ -\ 249 \\ \hline \end{array}$$

Step 2
Have your child complete problem A at the right. This problem may require additional steps. (These steps are outlined below.) Confirm that your child's answer is correct.

Additional Steps
1. Point out the zero in the tens column.
2. Ask, "How do I borrow from the tens when there's a zero in the tens column?" *(Borrow from the hundreds.)*
3. Borrow from the hundreds column.
4. Borrow from the tens column.

Sample Problem

H	T	O
⁴5̸	⁹1̸0̸	¹²2̸
− 2	4	7
2	5	5

Step 3
Have your child complete the remaining practice problems on his own.

Step 1 answer: 574

Target These!

A. $\begin{array}{r} 502 \\ -\ 247 \\ \hline \end{array}$ B. $\begin{array}{r} 704 \\ -\ 328 \\ \hline \end{array}$

Try using these steps!

C. $\begin{array}{r} 800 \\ -\ 241 \\ \hline \end{array}$ D. $\begin{array}{r} 207 \\ -\ 139 \\ \hline \end{array}$

E. $\begin{array}{r} 501 \\ -\ 265 \\ \hline \end{array}$ F. $\begin{array}{r} 903 \\ -\ 635 \\ \hline \end{array}$

G. $\begin{array}{r} 403 \\ -\ 187 \\ \hline \end{array}$

H. $\begin{array}{r} 702 \\ -\ 258 \\ \hline \end{array}$

Answers: 255, 376, 559, 68, 236, 268, 216, 444

If your child is quick to solve the remaining math problems correctly, an occasional review may be all he needs. But if several of the answers are incorrect, it's a good idea to spend some time each day having your child work through a problem or two at home until he's mastered this skill.

Checkup 8

Name _____ Date _____

A.	807 −719	907 −543	603 −328	402 −228	500 −469
B.	908 −319	604 −267	700 −414	300 −276	403 −355
C.	600 −182	405 −234	302 −196	700 −523	809 −296
D.	303 −245	500 −273	200 −144	901 −125	709 −353
E.	206 −128	404 −161	800 −565	305 −176	500 −387

Test A: 3 digits minus 3 digits with regrouping across zeros

©The Education Center, Inc. • *Target Math Success* • TEC60828 • Key p. 136

Checkup 8

Name _____ Date _____

A.	200 −135	904 −687	503 −149	705 −292	804 −457
B.	300 −256	200 −173	800 −163	406 −373	600 −528
C.	304 −269	708 −189	401 −272	900 −245	607 −129
D.	800 −366	203 −168	306 −167	504 −318	700 −624
E.	600 −431	501 −283	400 −247	203 −167	900 −464

Test A: 3 digits minus 3 digits with regrouping across zeros

©The Education Center, Inc. • *Target Math Success* • TEC60828 • Key p. 136

It's Time to Take Aim!

On _____ our class will be having a checkup on subtraction of larger numbers. To help your child prepare, please spend about 20 minutes reviewing math problems that involve **subtracting 3 digits from 4 digits with regrouping.** Thanks for your help!

Target These!

A.	3,257 − 478	B.	9,415 − 637
C.	7,369 − 517	D.	3,274 − 481
E.	5,264 − 528	F.	8,752 − 361
		G.	2,473 − 289
		H.	1,162 − 453

Subtraction Refresher

Step 1
Have your child complete the problem below. During a recent checkup, your child showed an understanding of this type of subtraction. Confirm that his answer is correct.

```
  846
− 459
```

Step 2
Have your child complete problem A at the right. This problem may require an additional step. (This step is outlined below.) Confirm that your child's answer is correct.

Additional Step
1. Bring down the number in the thousands column.

Th	H	T	O
²3̸	¹¹1̸2̸	¹⁴5̸	¹⁷7̸
−	4	7	8
2	7	7	9

Step 3
Have your child complete the remaining practice problems on his own.

Try using these steps!

Step 1 answer: 387

Answer: 2,779, 8,778, 6,852, 2,793, 4,736, 8,391, 2,184, 709

If your child is quick to solve the remaining math problems correctly, an occasional review may be all he needs. But if several of the answers are incorrect, it's a good idea to spend some time each day having your child work through a problem or two at home until he's mastered this skill.

118

Checkup 9

Name _____ Date _____

A.	4,349 − 583	3,612 − 457	5,456 − 782	9,374 − 849
B.	9,653 − 247	4,422 − 616	8,236 − 169	6,529 − 754
C.	4,231 − 956	7,614 − 845	1,598 − 669	2,246 − 858
D.	3,395 − 874	6,274 − 383	4,634 − 972	8,731 − 943
E.	5,382 − 692	3,132 − 479	7,272 − 851	6,532 − 954

Test A: 4 digits minus 3 digits with regrouping

©The Education Center, Inc. • *Target Math Success* • TEC60828 • Key p. 136

Checkup 9

Name _____ Date _____

A.	9,361 − 898	6,256 − 632	3,134 − 378	5,861 − 145	2,733 − 952
B.	3,713 − 826	7,175 − 937	4,261 − 987	6,327 − 944	8,252 − 195
C.	2,718 − 532	4,154 − 685	8,543 − 926	1,464 − 794	5,273 − 427
D.	7,456 − 962	2,476 − 187	9,732 − 958	4,516 − 248	6,378 − 439
E.	8,251 − 675	7,362 − 459	3,149 − 759	9,271 − 185	1,632 − 987

Test B: 4 digits minus 3 digits with regrouping

©The Education Center, Inc. • *Target Math Success* • TEC60828 • Key p. 136

It's Time to Take Aim!

On _____ our class will be having a checkup on subtraction of larger numbers. To help your child prepare, please spend about 20 minutes reviewing math problems that involve **subtracting 3 digits from 4 digits with regrouping across zeros.** Thanks for your help!

Target These!

A.	3,002	B.	7,048
	− 769		− 789

C.	6,700	D.	9,605
	− 857		− 957

E.	8,401	F.	5,006
	− 683		− 487

		G.	4,020
			− 2,459

		H.	9,040
			− 859

Subtraction Refresher

Step 1
Have your child complete the problem below. During a recent checkup, your child showed an understanding of this type of subtraction. Confirm that his answer is correct.

$$2,416 - 785$$

Step 2
Have your child complete problem A at the right. This problem may require an additional steps. (This step is outlined below.) Confirm that your child's answer is correct.

Additional Step
1. Subtract the numbers in the thousands column.

Th	H	T	O
$\overset{2}{\cancel{3}}$	$\overset{9}{\cancel{10}}\cancel{0}$	$\overset{9}{\cancel{10}}\cancel{0}$	$\overset{12}{\cancel{2}}$
−	7	6	9
2	2	3	3

Step 3
Have your child complete the remaining practice problems on his own.

Step 1 answer: 1,631

Try using these steps!

Answers: 2,233; 6,259; 5,843; 8,648; 7,718; 4,519; 3,561; 8,181

If your child is quick to solve the remaining math problems correctly, an occasional review may be all he needs. But if several of the answers are incorrect, it's a good idea to spend some time each day having your child work through a problem or two at home until he's mastered this skill.

Checkup 10

Name _____

Date _____

A.	7,104 − 677	9,063 − 975	8,400 − 684	4,026 − 149
B.	9,024 − 339	2,500 − 439	7,000 − 978	6,100 − 292
C.	8,020 − 686	8,000 − 489	7,103 − 717	4,013 − 837
D.	6,700 − 592	8,010 − 675	3,000 − 569	9,010 − 429
E.	6,000 − 516	7,600 − 359	5,070 − 894	9,000 − 786

Test A: 4 digits minus 3 digits with regrouping across zeros

©The Education Center, Inc. • *Target Math Success* • TEC60828 • Key p. 136

Checkup 10

Name _____

Date _____

A.	6,020 − 633	5,306 − 858	8,500 − 878	2,010 − 569	9,000 − 182
B.	4,604 − 885	9,020 − 568	5,500 − 759	8,202 − 575	7,001 − 994
C.	9,400 − 954	4,001 − 973	8,020 − 487	7,703 − 965	6,000 − 259
D.	3,103 − 245	7,900 − 248	8,040 − 857	5,000 − 678	9,601 − 994
E.	8,000 − 677	7,201 − 197	3,003 − 466	9,020 − 165	6,105 − 878

Test B: 4 digits minus 3 digits with regrouping across zeros

©The Education Center, Inc. • *Target Math Success* • TEC60828 • Key p. 136

Show Your Work

Name _____   Date _____

Show Your Work

Name _____ Date _____

Your subtraction skills are right on target!

_____
Student

_____
Teacher

_____
Date

Bull's-eye! Your subtraction skills have hit the target!

_____
Student

_____
Teacher

_____
Date

Rub-a-dub-dub

Subtract.
Color the bubble with the matching answer.

- $12 - 0 = 12$
- $48 - 1 = 47$
- $87 - 2 = 85$
- $24 - 3 = 21$
- $64 - 2 = 62$
- $55 - 4 = 51$
- $19 - 8 = 11$
- $72 - 1 = 71$
- $99 - 3 = 96$
- $36 - 1 = 35$
- $38 - 6 = 32$
- $26 - 4 = 22$
- $87 - 4 = 83$
- $57 - 7 = 50$

2 digits minus 1 digit without regrouping **7**

Fly Away Home

Subtract.
Help Lilly find her way home.
If the answer has a difference of less than 50, color the box red.

$39 - 4 = 35$	$56 - 5 = 51$	$63 - 3 = 60$	$84 - 2 = 82$	$75 - 2 = 73$
$42 - 1 = 41$	$78 - 6 = 72$	$17 - 1 = 16$	$29 - 2 = 27$	$36 - 1 = 35$
$18 - 6 = 12$	$93 - 1 = 92$	$35 - 2 = 33$	$69 - 7 = 62$	$28 - 2 = 26$
$46 - 4 = 42$	$14 - 0 = 14$	$27 - 3 = 24$	$88 - 4 = 84$	$45 - 4 = 41$

Ladybug Lane

10 2 digits minus 1 digit without regrouping

Art in Motion

Subtract.
Show your work.
Color by the code.

- $84 - 7 = 77$
- $81 - 8 = 73$
- $73 - 6 = 67$
- $43 - 9 = 34$
- $18 - 9 = 9$
- $52 - 7 = 45$
- $96 - 7 = 89$
- $75 - 6 = 69$
- $64 - 5 = 59$
- $47 - 9 = 38$
- $24 - 7 = 17$
- $41 - 5 = 36$
- $35 - 9 = 26$
- $92 - 4 = 88$
- $86 - 8 = 78$
- $98 - 9 = 89$

Color Code
0–35 = yellow
36–65 = red
66–95 = blue

2 digits minus 1 digit with regrouping **13**

Race to the Finish

Name _____ Date _____

Subtract.

- $36 - 5 = 31$
- $17 - 4 = 13$
- $85 - 1 = 84$
- $49 - 3 = 46$
- $64 - 2 = 62$
- $57 - 2 = 55$
- $76 - 4 = 72$
- $18 - 3 = 15$
- $28 - 6 = 22$
- $45 - 2 = 43$
- $88 - 4 = 84$
- $92 - 1 = 91$
- $29 - 6 = 23$
- $53 - 1 = 52$

8 2 digits minus 1 digit without regrouping

Penguins on Ice

Name _____ Date _____

Read.
Solve.
Show your work.

Petey spins 37 times on the ice. Patty spins 2 times. How many more times does Petey spin?

___35___ spins

On Monday, 76 penguins watched the show. On Tuesday, 5 penguins watched. How many more penguins watched on Monday?

___71___ penguins

68 penguins wave red scarves during the show. 6 penguins wave blue scarves. How many more penguins wave red scarves?

___62___ penguins

Peanut dives 59 times during the show. Pop dives 6 times. How many more times does Peanut dive?

___53___ dives

Patty skates for 45 minutes. Peanut skates for 3 minutes. How much longer does Patty skate?

___42___ minutes

After the show, Petey eats 27 fish. Peanut eats 2 fish. How many more fish does Petey eat?

___25___ fish

Story Problems **11**

Soaring Over the Bar

Name _____ Date _____

Subtract.
Show your work.
Cross off the answer.

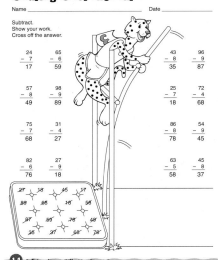

- $24 - 7 = 17$
- $65 - 6 = 59$
- $43 - 8 = 35$
- $96 - 9 = 87$
- $57 - 8 = 49$
- $98 - 9 = 89$
- $25 - 7 = 18$
- $72 - 4 = 68$
- $75 - 7 = 68$
- $31 - 4 = 27$
- $86 - 8 = 78$
- $54 - 9 = 45$
- $82 - 6 = 76$
- $27 - 9 = 18$
- $63 - 5 = 58$
- $45 - 8 = 37$

14 2 digits minus 1 digit with regrouping

Turn Up the Tunes!

Name _____ Date _____

Subtract.

What do you get when you cross a radio with a refrigerator?

$75 - 3 = 72$	$68 - 6 = 62$	$46 - 2 = 44$
A	U	E
$59 - 4 = 55$	$13 - 2 = 11$	$37 - 2 = 35$
M	R	S
$82 - 1 = 81$	$48 - 5 = 43$	$24 - 3 = 21$
O	I	L
$35 - 2 = 33$	$93 - 1 = 92$	$67 - 4 = 63$
C	Y	L
$76 - 2 = 74$	$57 - 5 = 52$	$88 - 3 = 85$
C	L	O

To solve the riddle, match the letters to the numbered lines below.

R E A L L Y   C O O L   M U S I C !
11 44 72 52 63 92   33 81 85 21   55 43 35 43 74

2 digits minus 1 digit without regrouping **9**

Keeping a Lookout

Name _____ Date _____

Subtract.
Show your work.

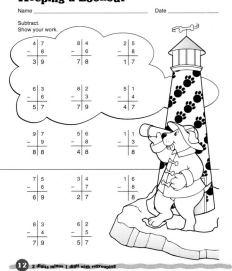

- $47 - 8 = 39$
- $84 - 6 = 78$
- $25 - 8 = 17$
- $63 - 6 = 57$
- $82 - 3 = 79$
- $51 - 4 = 47$
- $97 - 9 = 88$
- $56 - 8 = 48$
- $11 - 3 = 8$
- $75 - 6 = 69$
- $34 - 7 = 27$
- $83 - 4 = 79$
- $62 - 5 = 57$

12 2 digits minus 1 digit with regrouping

So Many Seashells

Subtract.
Show your work on another sheet of paper.
If the answer is correct, color the seashell.

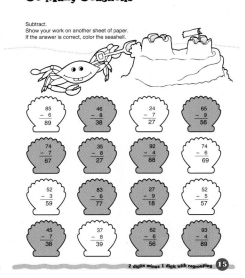

- $85 - 6 = 89$
- $46 - 8 = 38$
- $24 - 7 = 27$
- $65 - 9 = 56$
- $74 - 7 = 67$
- $35 - 8 = 27$
- $92 - 4 = 88$
- $74 - 6 = 69$
- $52 - 3 = 59$
- $83 - 6 = 77$
- $27 - 9 = 18$
- $52 - 5 = 57$
- $45 - 7 = 39$
- $37 - 8 = 39$
- $62 - 6 = 56$
- $93 - 4 = 89$

2 digits minus 1 digit with regrouping **15**

To Market, to Market

Name _____ Date _____

Read.
Solve.
Show your work.

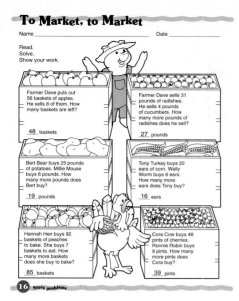

Farmer Dave puts out 56 baskets of apples. He sells 8 of them. How many baskets are left?

48 baskets

Farmer Dave sells 31 pounds of radishes. He sells 4 pounds of cucumbers. How many more pounds of radishes does he sell?

27 pounds

Bert Bear buys 25 pounds of potatoes. Millie Mouse buys 6 pounds. How many more pounds does Bert buy?

19 pounds

Tony Turkey buys 22 ears of corn. Wally Worm buys 6 ears. How many more ears are there Tony buy?

16 ears

Hannah Hen buys 92 baskets of peaches to bake. She buys 7 baskets to eat. How many more baskets does she buy to bake?

85 baskets

Cora Cow buys 48 pints of cherries. Ronnie Robin buys 9 pints. How many more pints does Cora buy?

39 pints

Shoe Shopping Spree

Name _____ Date _____

Help the chickens get to the shoe store.
Circle each correct fact.
Draw a line to connect the circled facts.

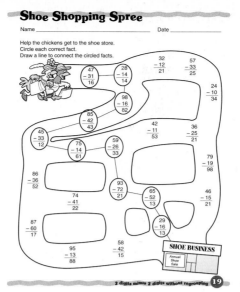

```
  47        32        57
 -31       -12       -33
  16        21        25
                              24
  98                         -10
 -16                          34
  82
  85
 -42        42        36
  43       -11       -25
  45        53        21
 -33
  12        75        59        79
           -14       -26       -19
  86        61        33        98
 -36
  52        74        93        65        46
           -41       -72       -52       -15
  87        22        21        13        21
 -60
  17                 29
                     -16
           95        13        58
          -13                 -42
           88        SHOE      15
                   BUSINESS
                  Annual
                  Shoe
                  Sale
```

Home Improvements

Name _____ Date _____

Read.
Solve.
Show your work.

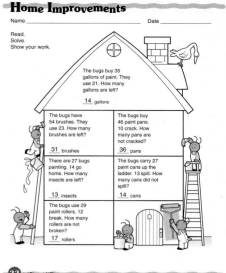

The bugs buy 35 gallons of paint. They use 21. How many gallons are left?

14 gallons

The bugs have 54 brushes. They use 23. How many brushes are left?

31 brushes

The bugs buy 46 paint pans. 10 crack. How many pans are not cracked?

36 pans

There are 27 bugs painting. 14 go home. How many insects are left?

13 insects

The bugs carry 27 paint cans up the ladder. 13 spill. How many cans did not spill?

14 cans

The bugs use 29 paint rollers. 12 break. How many rollers are not broken?

17 rollers

Doing the Burger Boogie

Name _____ Date _____

Subtract.
Show your work.

Where do hamburgers go when they want to dance?

38 −6 = 32	93 −1 = 92	26 −8 = 18	45 −2 = 43	63 −6 = 57	37 −2 = 35
Y	E	O	H	M	G
24 −7 = 17	87 −4 = 83	73 −6 = 67	76 −4 = 72	64 −2 = 62	45 −8 = 37
H	T	T	A	O	B
88 −3 = 85	75 −7 = 68	49 −3 = 46	96 −9 = 87	31 −4 = 27	57 −5 = 52
E	A	L	E	L	T

To solve the riddle above, match the letters to the numbered lines below.

T H E Y   G O   T O   T H E   M E A T   B A L L
67 17 92 32   35 62   67 18   52 43 87   57 85 68 83   37 72 27 46

Schooltime Jive

Name _____ Date _____

Subtract.
Color by the code.

Color Code	
10–20 = red	31–40 = blue
21–30 = green	41–50 = orange

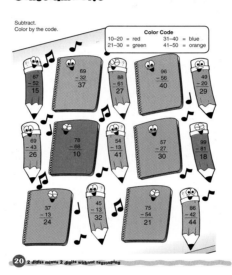

```
 67      69      96      49
-52     -32     -56     -20
 15      37      40      29

 69      78      54      57      99
-43     -68     -13     -27     -81
 26      10      41      30      18

 37      45      88      75      86
-13     -13     -54     -54     -42
 24      32      34      21      44
```

Computer Solutions

Name _____ Date _____

Subtract.
Show your work.

73 −46 = 27	35 −27 = 8	96 −38 = 58	58 −29 = 29	42 −37 = 5
26 −19 = 7	61 −25 = 36	24 −18 = 6	52 −37 = 15	85 −59 = 26
94 −67 = 27	47 −28 = 19	81 −43 = 38	73 −38 = 35	35 −16 = 19

Gumball Surprises

Name _____ Date _____

Subtract.
Color the gumball with the matching answer.

54 −31 = 23	38 −16 = 22
75 −40 = 35	26 −15 = 11
69 −42 = 27	85 −32 = 53
32 −11 = 21	74 −53 = 21
57 −... = 30	25 −12 = 13
93 −... = 31	49 −17 = 32

(gumballs: 21, 27, 23, 32, 30, 31, 11, 53, 52, 36, 22, 13, 21, 35)

67 −31 = 36   74 −22 = 52

Dragons Rule!

Name _____ Date _____

Subtract.
Cross off a matching answer.

DRAGONS RULE!

```
 31      90      97      67
-20     -70     -50     -42
 11      20      47      25

 47      86      79      35
-14     -76     -58     -12
 33      10      21      23

 49      54      67      28
-35     -22     -43     -11
 14      32      24      17

 99      38      74      85
-27     -16     -21     -23
 72      22      53      62
```

(column: 62 14 20 53 33 47 24 21 72 16 22 37 11 23 25)

Stargazers

Name _____ Date _____

Subtract.
Show your work.
Color the star with the matching answer.

```
 75      37
-46     -19
 29      18

 22              83
-17             -27
  5              56

 37      51      72      65
-18     -22     -34     -29
 19      29      38      36

 84      56      45      74
-68     -29     -18     -56
 16      27      27      18

 45      93      66      52
-18     -36     -37     -18
 27      57      29      34
```

Pond Pals

Name _____ Date _____

Subtract.
Show your work.
Connect the dots in order from least to greatest.

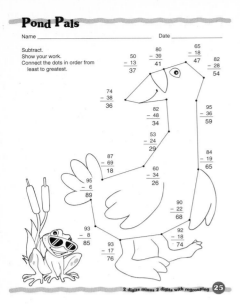

```
          65
          − 18
    80    47
    − 39        82
50  41         − 28
− 13            54
37
         82
74       − 48         95
− 38      34          − 36
36                    59
         53
         − 24
         29           84
87                    − 19
− 69     60           65
18       − 34
         26
95
− 6               90
89                − 22
93                68
− 8
85                92
93                − 18
− 17              74
76
```

Picture-Perfect?

Name _____ Date _____

Subtract.
Show your work on another sheet of paper.
If the answer is correct, color the photograph.

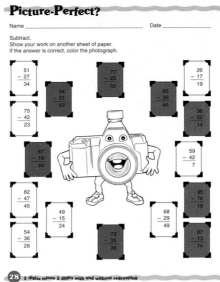

```
51        77              26
− 27      − 25            − 17
34        52              19

     94             85
     − 31           − 39
75   63             46      36
− 42                        − 14
23                          22

67                     59
− 18                   − 42
49                     7

82        49              95
− 47      − 15            − 76
45        24              19

54        73         68   87
− 36      − 35       − 29  − 13
28        38         49    74
```

Unwinding at the Web

Name _____ Date _____

Subtract.
Color by the code.

Color Code	
100–199 = blue	400–499 = yellow
200–299 = green	500–599 = orange
300–399 = red	600–699 = purple

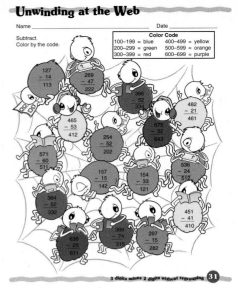

```
127      269          386
− 14     − 47         − 52        482
113      222          334        − 21
                                 461
         465
         − 53         254
         412          − 52
571                   202        675
− 60                             − 32
511      157          164        643
         − 15         − 33
         142          121        536
                                 − 24
384                              512
− 52
332      389          297        451
         − 74         − 32       − 41
636      315          282        410
− 25
611
```

Movie Munchies

Name _____ Date _____

Subtract.
Show your work.
Help Gus find his soda.
Color each popcorn tub with an even difference yellow.

```
95    27    40    98
− 36  − 18  − 11  − 49
59    9     29    49

60    51    30    83    50
− 24  − 27  − 12  − 26  − 25
36    24    18    57    25

32    74    43    52    64
− 19  − 17  − 25  − 35  − 29
13    57    18    17    35

87    91    75    60
− 48  − 24  − 37  − 18
39    67    38    42
```

Darting Dragonflies

Name _____ Date _____

Subtract.
Show your work.
Color each space with an even difference.

Dragonflies are the fastest insects. How many miles per hour do they fly?

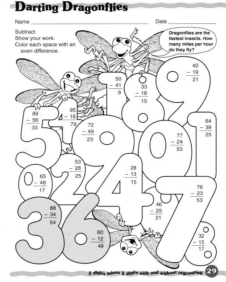

```
                         40
                         − 19
          50             21
          − 41    33
                  − 18
                  15
89
− 56
33        95             77
          − 16           − 24
          79    72       53
                − 49
                23
                         64
                         − 39
          53             25
          − 28
          25    28
                − 13
     65         15
     − 48                76
     17                  − 23
                         53
88                46
− 34              − 25
54                21     32
          60             − 15
          − 12           17
          48
```

Shootin' Hoops

Name _____ Date _____

Subtract.

427 − 13 = 414	651 − 30 = 621	175 − 22 = 153	295 − 74 = 221	562 − 30 = 532	385 − 44 = 341	721 − 20 = 701
B	T	U	O	H	L	E
965 − 42 = 923	458 − 31 = 427	634 − 23 = 611	879 − 48 = 831	275 − 31 = 244	994 − 62 = 932	647 − 25 = 622
E	B	E	L	A	H	G
397 − 46 = 351	625 − 15 = 610	284 − 61 = 223	798 − 57 = 741			
C	Y	A	H			
179 − 46 = 133	545 − 43 = 502	886 − 43 = 843				
S	E	T				

Why can't you play basketball with pigs?
To solve the riddle, match the letters to the numbered lines below.

```
B  E  C  A  U  S  E        T  H  E  Y
414 502 351 244 153 133 923   621 532 701 610

H  O  G        T  H  E        B  A  L  L !
932 221 622   843 741 611   427 223 831 341
```

A Good Day for Golf

Name _____ Date _____

Read.
Subtract.
Show your work.

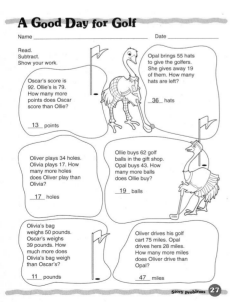

Oscar's score is 92. Ollie's is 79. How many more points does Oscar score than Ollie?
___13___ points

Opal brings 55 hats to give to the golfers. She gives away 19 of them. How many hats are left?
___36___ hats

Oliver plays 34 holes. Olivia plays 17. How many more holes does Oliver play than Olivia?
___17___ holes

Ollie buys 62 golf balls in the gift shop. Opal buys 43. How many more balls does Ollie buy?
___19___ balls

Olivia's bag weighs 50 pounds. Oscar's weighs 39 pounds. How much more does Olivia's bag weigh than Oscar's?
___11___ pounds

Oliver drives his golf cart 75 miles. Opal drives hers 28 miles. How many more miles does Oliver drive than Opal?
___47___ miles

Let's Eat!

Name _____ Date _____

Subtract.
Circle each matching answer in the picture.

```
563    279    421    386    575
− 41   − 58   − 10   − 42   − 34
522    221    411    344    541

671    297    654    383    294
− 20   − 44   − 32   − 21   − 62
651    253    622    362    232

197    460    730    125    615
− 31   − 20   − 20   − 12   − 13
166    440    710    113    602
```

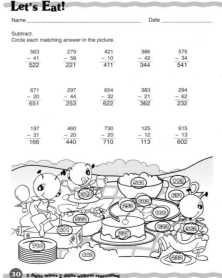

Look Whooo's at the Library!

Name _____ Date _____

Subtract.
Color by the code.

Color Code	
100–250 = yellow	
251–400 = blue	
401–550 = green	
551–700 = red	
701–950 = brown	

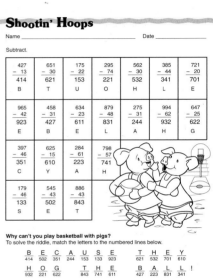

```
827     465    384    270          135
− 14    − 30   − 63   − 30         − 23
813     435    321    240          112

973   194   684   265    929   593   524   279
− 31  − 32  − 61  − 14   − 16   − 33  − 13  − 25
162         623   251    913   560   511   254
                  314

                           166
                           − 25
                           141

464                     758   842   954
− 42                    − 31   − 10   − 22
422                     727   832   932

                637
                − 25
                612
```

Leo's Sweet Treats

Name _____ Date _____

Read.
Solve.
Show your work.

Leo has 178 gumdrops. He sells 46. How many gumdrops are left? __132__ gumdrops	There are 256 suckers on a tray. Leo moves 35 to a jar. How many suckers are left on the tray? __221__ suckers
Leo sells 454 chocolates on Monday. That is 21 more than he sells on Tuesday. How many chocolates does he sell on Tuesday? __433__ chocolates	Leo has 748 caramels. 26 melt. How many caramels are left? __722__ caramels
Leo sells 672 sour balls and 51 gumdrops. How many more sour balls does he sell? __621__ sour balls	Leo has 497 jelly beans. 84 are red and the rest are green. How many jelly beans are green? __413__ green

---

Fun Fishing Buddies

Subtract.
Help Frank find his fishing buddy.
Use a green crayon to color each box with a difference of less than 100.

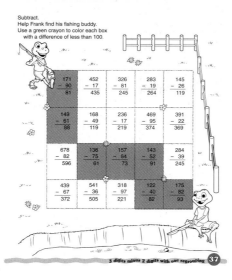

171 − 90 = 81	452 − 17 = 435	326 − 81 = 245	283 − 19 = 264	145 − 26 = 119
149 − 61 = 88	168 − 49 = 119	236 − 17 = 219	469 − 95 = 374	391 − 22 = 369
678 − 82 = 596	136 − 75 = 61	157 − 84 = 73	143 − 52 = 91	284 − 39 = 245
439 − 67 = 372	541 − 36 = 505	318 − 97 = 221	122 − 40 = 82	175 − 82 = 93

Moving Day

Name _____ Date _____

Subtract.
Show your work.

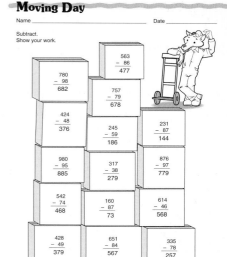

563 − 86 = 477

780 − 98 = 682

757 − 79 = 678

424 − 48 = 376

245 − 59 = 186

231 − 87 = 144

980 − 95 = 885

317 − 38 = 279

876 − 97 = 779

542 − 74 = 468

160 − 87 = 73

614 − 46 = 568

428 − 49 = 379

651 − 84 = 567

335 − 78 = 257

Excellent Exercise!

Name _____ Date _____

Subtract.

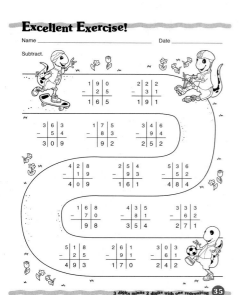

190 − 25 = 165

222 − 31 = 191

363 − 54 = 309

175 − 83 = 92

346 − 94 = 252

428 − 19 = 409

254 − 93 = 161

536 − 52 = 484

168 − 70 = 98

435 − 81 = 354

353 − 82 = 271

518 − 25 = 493

261 − 91 = 170

303 − 61 = 242

The Ice-Cream Counter

Name _____ Date _____

Read.
Solve.
Show your work.

Two Scoops $1.00

The jar has 396 sprinkles. Bessie uses 27 sprinkles. How many sprinkles are left? __369__ sprinkles	Bessie leaves 428 ice-cream sandwiches by the window. 36 of them melt. How many ice-cream sandwiches are left? __392__ ice-cream sandwiches
The store has 564 ice-cream cones. Bessie uses 35 cones in one day. How many cones are left? __529__ cones	Bessie makes 473 gallons of ice cream. She sells 91 gallons. How many gallons are left? __382__ gallons
Bessie makes 681 milk shakes in a month. 72 of the milk shakes are vanilla. How many are not vanilla? __609__ milk shakes	Bessie has 835 jars of hot fudge. She uses 41 of them. How many jars of hot fudge are left? __794__ jars

---

Light Up the Night!

Name _____ Date _____

Subtract.
Show your work on another sheet of paper.
If the answer is correct, color the burst red.

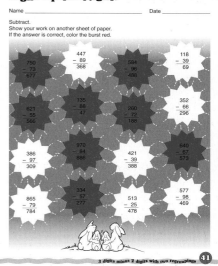

750 − 73 = 677

447 − 89 = 368

584 − 96 = 488

118 − 39 = 69

621 − 55 = 566

135 − 88 = 47

260 − 72 = 188

352 − 66 = 296

386 − 97 = 309

970 − 84 = 886

421 − 39 = 388

640 − 67 = 573

865 − 79 = 784

334 − 57 = 277

513 − 25 = 478

577 − 98 = 469

Paulie Wants a Pizza!

Name _____ Date _____

Subtract.
Cross off the answer.

Paulie's Pizzeria

331
118
170
474
609

549 − 98 = 451

491 − 63 = 428

347 − 60 = 287

529 − 55 = 474

418 − 88 = 330

325 − 34 = 291

534 − 18 = 516

462 − 71 = 391

276 − 84 = 192

284 − 57 = 227

325 − 93 = 232

183 − 65 = 118

279 − 94 = 185

231 − 61 = 170

556 − 28 = 528

437 − 87 = 350

568 − 59 = 509

353 − 19 = 334

185   192   330
287   528   461
232   516   391
350   516
428   227

Make a Wish

Name _____ Date _____

Subtract.
Show your work.

962 − 85 = 877

345 − 89 = 256

635 − 98 = 537

773 − 86 = 687

621 − 36 = 585

563 − 74 = 489

840 − 77 = 763

254 − 67 = 187

940 − 63 = 877

432 − 77 = 355

761 − 94 = 667

327 − 49 = 278

553 − 88 = 465

576 − 88 = 489

Assorted Chocolates

Name _____ Date _____

Read.
Solve.
Show your work.

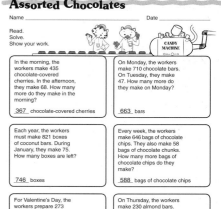

CANDY MACHINE

In the morning, the workers make 435 chocolate-covered cherries. In the afternoon, they make 68. How many more do they make in the morning? __367__ chocolate-covered cherries	On Monday, the workers make 710 chocolate bars. On Tuesday, they make 47. How many more do they make on Monday? __663__ bars
Each year, the workers must make 821 boxes of coconut bars. During January, they make 75. How many boxes are left? __746__ boxes	Every week, the workers make 646 bags of chocolate chips. They also make 58 bags of chocolate chunks. How many more bags of chocolate chips do they make? __588__ bags of chocolate chips
For Valentine's Day, the workers prepare 273 heart-shaped boxes. They ship 96 boxes right away. How many boxes are left? __177__ boxes	On Thursday, the workers make 230 almond bars. On Friday, they ship 92 almond bars. How many are left? __138__ bars

Digging Up Diamonds

Name _____ Date _____

Subtract.
Circle the answers that are odd.
Connect the circled answers to help
Grover find the diamonds.

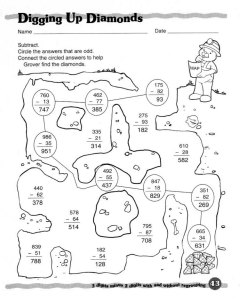

(760 − 13 = 747)   (462 − 77 = 385)   175 − 82 = 93

(986 − 35 = 951)   335 − 21 = 314   275 − 93 = 182

440 − 62 = 378   (492 − 55 = 437)   847 − 18 = 829   610 − 28 = 582

578 − 64 = 514   (351 − 82 = 269)

839 − 51 = 788   182 − 54 = 128   795 − 87 = 708   665 − 34 = 631

3 digits minus 2 digits with and without regrouping **43**

Hamster Hideaway

Name _____ Date _____

Subtract.
Cross off the answer on the wheel.

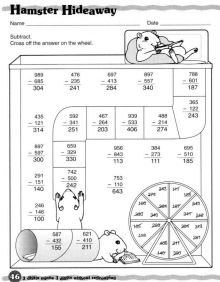

| 989 − 685 = 304 | 476 − 235 = 241 | 697 − 413 = 284 | 897 − 557 = 340 | 788 − 601 = 187 |

365 − 122 = 243

435 − 121 = 314   592 − 341 = 251   467 − 264 = 203   939 − 533 = 406   488 − 214 = 274

897 − 597 = 300   659 − 329 = 330   956 − 843 = 113   384 − 273 = 111   695 − 510 = 185

291 − 151 = 140   742 − 500 = 242   753 − 110 = 643

246 − 146 = 100

587 − 432 = 155   621 − 410 = 211

46 *3 digits minus 3 digits without regrouping*

Lunch Line

Name _____ Date _____

Read.
Solve.
Show your work.

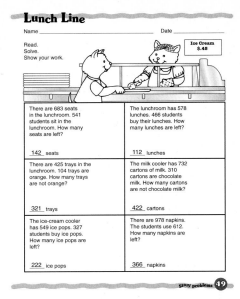

Ice Cream $.45

There are 683 seats in the lunchroom. 541 students sit in the lunchroom. How many seats are left?

__142__ seats

The lunchroom has 578 lunches. 466 students buy their lunches. How many lunches are left?

__112__ lunches

There are 425 trays in the lunchroom. 104 trays are orange. How many trays are not orange?

__321__ trays

The milk cooler has 732 cartons of milk. 310 cartons are chocolate milk. How many cartons are not chocolate milk?

__422__ cartons

The ice-cream cooler has 549 ice pops. 327 students buy ice pops. How many ice pops are left?

__222__ ice pops

There are 978 napkins. The students use 612. How many napkins are left?

__366__ napkins

Story problems **49**

Perfectly Square

Name _____ Date _____

Subtract.
Show your work.
Use your answers to complete each number puzzle.

Across
A. 284 − 42 = 242   D. 582 − 19 = 563   E. 844 − 97 = 747

Down
A. 320 − 63 = 257   B. 516 − 52 = 464   C. 253 − 16 = 237

A 2	B 4	C 2
D 5	6	3
G 7	4	7

Across
F. 840 − 46 = 794   I. 385 − 52 = 333   J. 423 − 75 = 348

Down
F. 815 − 82 = 733   G. 975 − 41 = 934   H. 497 − 59 = 438

F 7	G 9	H 4
I 3	3	3
J 3	4	8

Across
K. 756 − 24 = 732   N. 640 − 78 = 562   O. 193 − 47 = 146

Down
K. 850 − 99 = 751   L. 389 − 25 = 364   M. 317 − 91 = 226

K 7	L 3	M 2
N 5	6	2
O 1	4	6

44 *3 digits minus 2 digits with and without regrouping*

Running to the Oasis

Subtract.
Show your work on another sheet of paper.
Help Rudy Roadrunner find the oasis.
If the answer is correct, color the box.

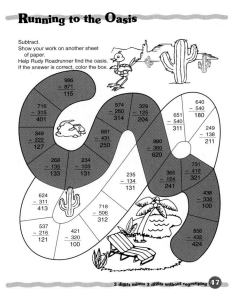

986 − 871 = 115
716 − 315 = 401   574 − 260 = 314   329 − 125 = 204   640 − 540 = 180
349 − 222 = 127   681 − 431 = 250   651 − 540 = 311   249 − 138 = 211
268 − 135 = 133   234 − 103 = 131   980 − 360 = 620
624 − 311 = 413   235 − 134 = 131   365 − 124 = 241   731 − 410 = 321
537 − 216 = 121   718 − 506 = 312   421 − 320 = 100   438 − 338 = 100   856 − 432 = 424

3 digits minus 3 digits without regrouping **47**

Under the Big Top

Name _____ Date _____

Subtract.
Show your work.

711 − 260 = 451   582 − 337 = 245   627 − 463 = 164   936 − 428 = 508

264 − 159 = 105   570 − 180 = 390   629 − 357 = 272   483 − 256 = 227

746 − 462 = 284   595 − 326 = 269   869 − 475 = 394   798 − 539 = 259

3 digits minus 3 digits with one regrouping **50**

What's for Lunch?

Name _____ Date _____

Subtract.
Color by the code.

Color Code
Between 200–299 = red
Between 300–399 = yellow
Between 400–499 = green

485 − 230 = 255   643 − 413 = 230   375 − 165 = 210   728 − 526 = 202

618 − 318 = 300   999 − 600 = 399   767 − 334 = 433   560 − 110 = 450

560 − 360 = 200   439 − 217 = 222   994 − 773 = 221   799 − 501 = 298

898 − 540 = 358   787 − 412 = 375   676 − 275 = 401   989 − 501 = 488

3 digits minus 3 digits without regrouping **45**

Chew Toy

Name _____ Date _____

Subtract.
Color by the code.

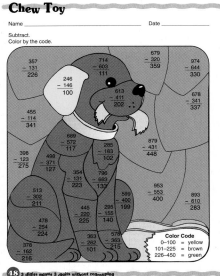

357 − 131 = 226   714 − 603 = 111   679 − 320 = 359   974 − 644 = 330

246 − 146 = 100   613 − 411 = 202   678 − 341 = 337

455 − 114 = 341   689 − 572 = 117   285 − 183 = 102   879 − 431 = 448

398 − 123 = 275   498 − 371 = 127   354 − 131 = 223   798 − 663 = 135   953 − 553 = 400

513 − 302 = 211   445 − 220 = 225   295 − 155 = 140   599 − 400 = 199   893 − 610 = 283

478 − 254 = 224   363 − 262 = 101   578 − 363 = 215

378 − 162 = 216

Color Code
0–100 = yellow
101–225 = brown
226–450 = green

48 *3 digits minus 3 digits without regrouping*

Beaver on Board

Name _____ Date _____

Subtract.
Show your work.
Color by the code.

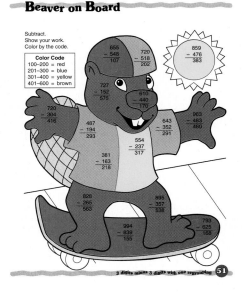

Color Code
100–200 = red
201–300 = blue
301–400 = yellow
401–600 = brown

655 − 548 = 107   720 − 518 = 202   859 − 476 = 383

727 − 152 = 575   610 − 440 = 170

720 − 304 = 416   487 − 194 = 293   643 − 352 = 291   963 − 483 = 480

554 − 237 = 317

381 − 163 = 218

826 − 265 = 563   895 − 357 = 538

994 − 839 = 155   793 − 625 = 168

3 digits minus 3 digits with one regrouping **51**

Play Ball!

Name _____ Date _____

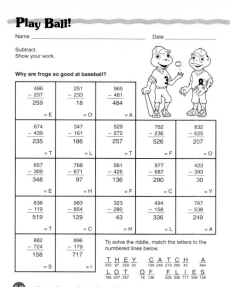

Subtract.
Show your work.

Why are frogs so good at baseball?

496 − 237 = 259 = E	251 − 233 = 18 = O	965 − 481 = 484 = A

674 − 439 = 235 = T	347 − 161 = 186 = L	529 − 272 = 257 = T	762 − 236 = 526 = F	832 − 625 = 207 = O

657 − 309 = 348 = E	768 − 671 = 97 = H	561 − 425 = 136 = F	977 − 687 = 290 = C	423 − 393 = 30 = Y

638 − 119 = 519 = T	983 − 854 = 129 = C	323 − 280 = 43 = H	494 − 158 = 336 = L	787 − 538 = 249 = A

882 − 724 = 158 = S	896 − 179 = 717 = I

To solve the riddle, match the letters to the numbered lines below.

T H E Y   C A T C H   A
235 97 259 30   129 249 519 290 43   484

L O T   O F   F L I E S
186 207 257   18 30   206 717 348 158

Cactus Calculations

Name _____ Date _____

Subtract.
Show your work.

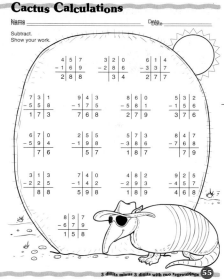

457 − 169 = 288	320 − 286 = 34	614 − 337 = 277

731 − 558 = 173	943 − 175 = 768	860 − 581 = 279	532 − 156 = 376

670 − 594 = 76	255 − 198 = 57	573 − 386 = 187	847 − 768 = 79

313 − 225 = 88	740 − 142 = 598	482 − 293 = 189	925 − 457 = 468

837 − 679 = 158

Just Ripe!

Subtract.
Show your work.
Color the apple with the matching answer.

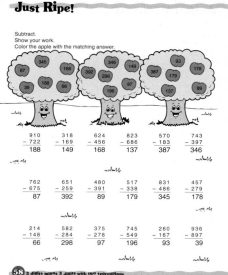

Apple trees with: 345, 168, 188, 39, 66 / 392, 346, 298, 149, 196, 97 / 93, 387, 179, 178, 89, 137

910 − 722 = 188	318 − 169 = 149	624 − 456 = 168	823 − 686 = 137	570 − 183 = 387	743 − 397 = 346

762 − 675 = 87	651 − 259 = 392	480 − 391 = 89	517 − 338 = 179	831 − 486 = 345	457 − 279 = 178

214 − 148 = 66	582 − 284 = 298	375 − 278 = 97	745 − 549 = 196	260 − 167 = 93	936 − 897 = 39

Lots of Lava

Subtract.
Show your work.
Color a matching answer.

Lava droplets: 219, 293, 91, 193, 181, 119, 108, 396, 384, 447, 46, 273, 16, 382, 105, 273, 273, 304, 619, 308

643 − 350 = 293	776 − 329 = 447	548 − 275 = 273

627 − 319 = 308	568 − 172 = 396	365 − 274 = 91	846 − 738 = 108

958 − 576 = 382	729 − 456 = 273	728 − 109 = 619	614 − 230 = 384	697 − 578 = 119	751 − 705 = 46

327 − 146 = 181	992 − 688 = 304	970 − 954 = 16	456 − 183 = 273	964 − 859 = 105	385 − 192 = 193	467 − 248 = 219

Pipin' Hot!

Name _____ Date _____

Subtract.
Show your work.

Pizza problems:
- 720 − 385 = 335
- 348 − 289 = 59
- 453 − 176 = 277
- 817 − 698 = 119
- 375 − 298 = 77
- 640 − 575 = 65
- 594 − 398 = 196
- 461 − 175 = 286
- 725 − 189 = 536
- 980 − 291 = 689
- 853 − 385 = 468
- 536 − 257 = 279
- 227 − 139 = 88
- 616 − 117 = 499
- 932 − 556 = 376
- 752 − 468 = 284

School's in Session

Name _____ Date _____

Read.
Solve.
Show your work.

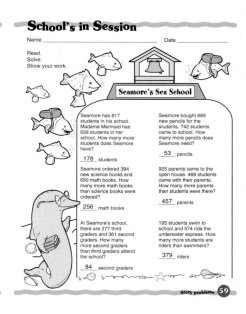

Seamore's Sea School

Seamore has 817 students in his school. Madame Mermaid has 639 students in her school. How many more students does Seamore have?

__178__ students

Seamore bought 689 new pencils for the students. 742 students came to school. How many more pencils does Seamore need?

__53__ pencils

Seamore ordered 394 new science books and 650 math books. How many more math books than science books were ordered?

__256__ math books

925 parents came to the open house. 468 students came with their parents. How many more parents than students were there?

__457__ parents

At Seamore's school, there are 277 third graders and 361 second graders. How many more second graders than third graders attend the school?

__84__ second graders

195 students swim to school and 574 ride the underwater express. How many more students are riders than swimmers?

__379__ riders

At the Museum

Name _____ Date _____

Read.
Solve.
Show your work.

There are 834 pictures. 272 have frames. The rest do not. How many pictures do not have frames?

__562__ pictures

The museum has 284 paintings. 109 are oil paintings and the rest are watercolor. How many watercolor paintings are there?

__175__ watercolor paintings

There are 681 visitors in the museum. 265 go home. How many visitors are left?

__416__ visitors

There are 559 statues in the museum. 264 are made of marble and the rest are made of stone. How many statues are made of stone?

__295__ stone statues

There are 723 paintings of animals. 182 are of horses. How many paintings are not of horses?

__541__ paintings

There are 712 steps in the museum. If a visitor climbs 450 steps, how many are left?

__262__ steps

Birds on a Wire

Subtract.
Show your work.
Color by the code.

Color Code
0–199 = red   400–599 = green
200–399 = blue   600–899 = yellow

426 − 379 = 47	921 − 143 = 778	483 − 195 = 288	752 − 287 = 465
516 − 298 = 218	640 − 586 = 54	738 − 139 = 599	850 − 697 = 153
941 − 254 = 687	716 − 249 = 467	815 − 387 = 428	563 − 167 = 396
662 − 289 = 373	872 − 184 = 688	220 − 175 = 45	934 − 179 = 755

Lounging Lobster

Subtract.
Show your work.
Color the music note with the correct answer.

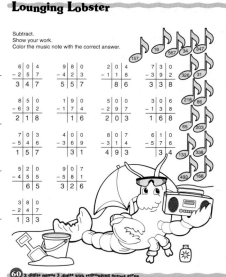

Music notes: 157, 16, 567, 34, 347, 326, 31, 218, 86, 65, 203, 133, 336, 493, 166

604 − 257 = 347	980 − 423 = 557	204 − 118 = 86	730 − 392 = 338
850 − 632 = 218	100 − 174 = 16	500 − 297 = 203	306 − 138 = 168
703 − 546 = 157	400 − 369 = 31	807 − 493 = 314	610 − 576 = 34
520 − 455 = 65	907 − 581 = 326		
380 − 247 = 133			

Up, Up, and Away

Name _____ Date _____

Subtract.
Show your work.
Color by the code.

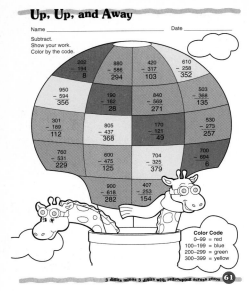

202 − 194 = 8	880 − 586 = 294	420 − 317 = 103	610 − 258 = 352
950 − 594 = 356	190 − 162 = 28	840 − 569 = 271	503 − 368 = 135
301 − 189 = 112	805 − 437 = 368	170 − 121 = 49	530 − 273 = 257
760 − 531 = 229	600 − 475 = 125	704 − 325 = 379	700 − 694 = 6
900 − 618 = 282	407 − 253 = 154		

Color Code
0–99 = red
100–199 = blue
200–299 = green
300–399 = yellow

Fairground Follies

Name _____ Date _____

Read.
Solve.
Show your work.

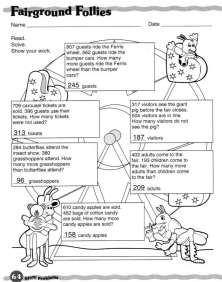

807 guests ride the Ferris wheel. 562 guests ride the bumper cars. How many more guests ride the Ferris wheel than the bumper cars?

245 guests

709 carousel tickets are sold. 396 guests use their tickets. How many tickets were not used?

313 tickets

284 butterflies attend the insect show. 380 grasshoppers attend. How many more grasshoppers than butterflies attend?

96 grasshoppers

317 visitors see the giant pig before the fair closes. 504 visitors are in line. How many visitors do not see the pig?

187 visitors

402 adults come to the fair. 193 children come to the fair. How many more adults than children come to the fair?

209 adults

610 candy apples are sold. 452 bags of cotton candy are sold. How many more candy apples are sold?

158 candy apples

Off to the Water Park

Name _____ Date _____

Subtract.
Show your work.

1 5 6 4 − 3 7 7 = 1 1 8 7	6 6 1 7 − 2 3 4 = 6 3 8 3	3 5 3 8 − 6 2 4 = 2 9 1 4
8 6 2 2 − 3 2 3 = 8 2 9 9	3 4 5 4 − 8 7 3 = 2 5 8 1	7 4 3 7 − 6 8 5 = 6 7 5 2
7 2 8 7 − 8 2 5 = 6 4 6 2	9 7 4 2 − 6 5 1 = 9 0 9 1	4 2 7 6 − 4 3 5 = 3 8 4 1
5 8 2 4 − 5 6 9 = 5 2 5 5		1 6 5 7 − 4 2 9 = 1 2 2 8
8 3 7 5 − 1 2 8 = 8 2 4 7		

Wiggle Water Park

Hat Trick

Name _____ Date _____

Subtract.
Show your work.
Write the matching letters from the code.
Read the riddle answer.

What did the hat say to the hat rack?

Code
18 = A
35 = R
62 = N
107 = H
126 = G
134 = S
171 = T
186 = O
254 = E
375 = L
429 = Y
464 = T
612 = I

390 − 256 = 134	850 − 386 = 464	407 − 389 = 18	700 − 271 = 429
S	T	A	Y

360 − 253 = 107	802 − 548 = 254	170 − 135 = 35	480 − 226 = 254
H	E	R	E

740 − 128 = 612	530 − 155 = 375	906 − 531 = 375		305 − 179 = 126	900 − 714 = 186
I	L	L		G	O

603 − 417 = 186	208 − 146 = 62	510 − 492 = 18	901 − 794 = 107	703 − 449 = 254	602 − 584 = 18	500 − 329 = 171
O	N		A	H	E	A D.

Far Out!

Name _____ Date _____

Subtract.
Show your work.
Color by the code.

Color Code
regrouping = red
no regrouping = yellow

476 − 202 = 274		
624 − 345 = 279	524 − 362 = 162	
553 − 291 = 262	806 − 579 = 227	
601 − 564 = 37	278 − 143 = 135	
385 − 196 = 189	622 − 459 = 163	
567 − 325 = 242	364 − 227 = 137	292 − 170 = 122
738 − 405 = 333	202 − 197 = 5	

High-Flying Fun

Name _____ Date _____

Subtract.
Show your work on another sheet of paper.
Color each trapeze that has the correct answer.

2,764 − 158 = 2,606	3,621 − 314 = 3,313	1,304 − 533 = 771	6,254 − 735 = 5,519	4,291 − 931 = 5,222
5,254 − 321 = 4,933	9,493 − 675 = 8,828	8,932 − 172 = 8,760	5,627 − 155 = 4,472	4,469 − 488 = 3,987
6,215 − 651 = 6,564	7,257 − 847 = 6,410	7,429 − 246 = 7,183	2,798 − 459 = 2,339	8,891 − 629 = 9,520
3,217 − 766 = 2,451	9,254 − 167 = 9,387	1,731 − 323 = 1,418	3,854 − 289 = 3,565	5,180 − 252 = 4,928

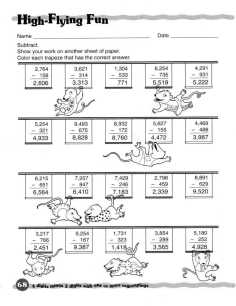

Sylvester's Steps

Name _____ Date _____

Subtract.
Show your work.
Help Sylvester climb up the mountain.
If the answer is even, color the rock brown.

Rocky Ridge

706 − 341 = 365	210 − 153 = 57	807 − 455 = 352
440 − 215 = 225	160 − 136 = 24	608 − 412 = 196	350 − 332 = 18	730 − 283 = 447
802 − 649 = 153	910 − 328 = 582	520 − 267 = 253	501 − 466 = 35	600 − 329 = 271
900 − 781 = 119	603 − 271 = 332	870 − 173 = 697	580 − 195 = 385	
405 − 317 = 88	704 − 694 = 10	990 − 838 = 152		

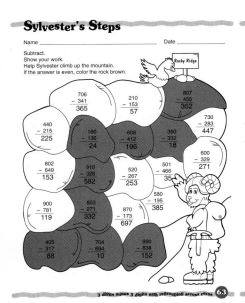

Marching Monsters

Name _____ Date _____

Subtract.
Show your work.
Cross off the matching answer.

272 18 179 113 36 189 426 281 155 177 218 168 223 155 248 143

468 − 325 = 143	625 − 407 = 218	461 − 293 = 168	264 − 139 = 125
387 − 198 = 189	402 − 384 = 18	942 − 661 = 281	259 − 146 = 113
423 − 165 = 258	597 − 374 = 223	677 − 498 = 179	905 − 728 = 177
807 − 559 = 248	753 − 327 = 426	523 − 368 = 155	829 − 557 = 272

Hop on Over!

Name _____ Date _____

Subtract.
Show your work.
Help the grasshopper get across the stream.
If the answer is odd, color the stone brown.

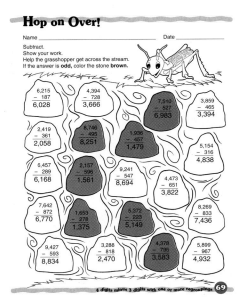

6,215 − 187 = 6,028	4,394 − 728 = 3,666	7,510 − 527 = 6,983	3,859 − 465 = 3,394
2,419 − 361 = 2,058	8,746 − 495 = 8,251	1,936 − 457 = 1,479	5,154 − 316 = 4,838
6,457 − 289 = 6,168	2,157 − 596 = 1,561	9,241 − 547 = 8,694	4,473 − 651 = 3,822
7,642 − 872 = 6,770	1,653 − 278 = 1,375	5,372 − 223 = 5,149	8,269 − 833 = 7,436
9,427 − 593 = 8,834	3,288 − 818 = 2,470	4,378 − 795 = 3,583	5,899 − 967 = 4,932

Digging Dinosaur

Name _____ Date _____

Subtract.
Show your work.
Cross off the matching answer on the rocks.

1,913 − 127 **1,786**	2,428 − 291 **2,137**	3,535 − 590 **2,945**	4,460 − 909 **3,551**
3,253 − 846 **2,407**	8,740 − 244 **8,496**	9,147 − 913 **8,234**	8,678 − 691 **7,987**	9,189 − 758 **8,431**
1,680 − 790 **890**	3,221 − 638 **2,583**	4,832 − 757 **4,075**	1,435 − 547 **888**
1,163 − 179 **984**	1,254 − 646 **608**	8,585 − 467 **8,118**	3,929 − 431 **3,498**
3,440 − 194 **3,246**	9,189 − 361 **8,828**	5,810 − 320 **5,490**

Rocks: 2,137 · 984 · 1,786 · 5,490 · 888 · 4,075 · 2,583 · 2,407 · 890 · 3,551 · 8,234 · 8,828 · 2,945 · 8,496 · 8,118 · 3,498 · 3,246 · 7,987 · 8,431

70 4 digits minus 3 digits with one or more regroupings

One Lucky Find

Name _____ Date _____

Subtract.
Show your work.
Color the coin with the matching answer.

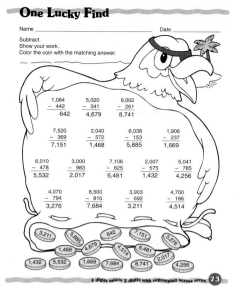

1,084 − 442 **642**	5,020 − 341 **4,679**	9,002 − 261 **8,741**
7,520 − 369 **7,151**	2,040 − 572 **1,468**	6,038 − 153 **5,885**	1,906 − 237 **1,669**
6,010 − 478 **5,532**	3,000 − 983 **2,017**	7,106 − 625 **6,481**	2,007 − 575 **1,432**	5,041 − 785 **4,256**
4,070 − 794 **3,276**	8,500 − 816 **7,684**	3,903 − 692 **3,211**	4,700 − 186 **4,514**

Coins: 3,211 · 5,885 · 642 · 7,151 · 3,276 · 1,468 · 4,679 · 4,514 · 6,481 · 2,017 · 1,432 · 5,532 · 1,669 · 7,684 · 8,741 · 4,256

73 4 digits minus 3 digits with regrouping across zeros

A Busy Place

Name _____ Date _____

Read.
Solve.
Show your work.

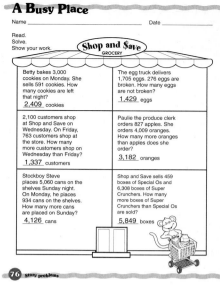

Shop and $ave GROCERY

Betty bakes 3,000 cookies on Monday. She sells 591 cookies. How many cookies are left that night? **2,409** cookies	The egg truck delivers 1,705 eggs. 276 eggs are broken. How many eggs are not broken? **1,429** eggs
2,100 customers shop at Shop and Save on Wednesday. On Friday, 763 customers shop at the store. How many more customers shop on Wednesday than Friday? **1,337** customers	Paulie the produce clerk orders 827 apples. She orders 4,009 oranges. How many more oranges than apples does she order? **3,182** oranges
Stockboy Steve places 5,060 cans on the shelves. On Monday, he places 934 cans on the shelves. How many more cans are placed on Sunday? **4,126** cans	Shop and Save sells 459 boxes of Special Os and 6,308 boxes of Super Crunchers. How many more boxes of Super Crunchers than Special Os are sold? **5,849** boxes

76 Story problems

Gas Up and Go!

Name _____ Date _____

Read.
Solve.
Show your work.

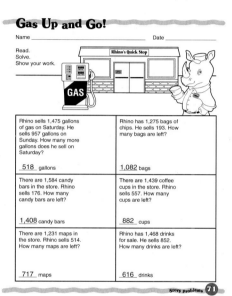

Rhino's Quick Stop **GAS**

Rhino sells 1,475 gallons of gas on Saturday. He sells 957 gallons on Sunday. How many more gallons does he sell on Saturday? **518** gallons	Rhino has 1,275 bags of chips. He sells 193. How many bags are left? **1,082** bags
There are 1,584 candy bars in the store. Rhino sells 176. How many candy bars are left? **1,408** candy bars	There are 1,439 coffee cups in the store. Rhino sells 557. How many cups are left? **882** cups
There are 1,231 maps in the store. Rhino sells 514. How many maps are left? **717** maps	Rhino has 1,468 drinks for sale. He sells 852. How many drinks are left? **616** drinks

71 Story problems

The Perfect Combination

Name _____ Date _____

Subtract.
Show your work.
Use your answers to complete the puzzles.

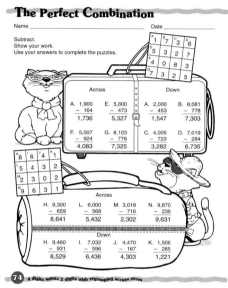

Across

A. 1,900
− 164
1,736   E. 5,800
− 473
5,327

F. 5,007
− 924
4,083   G. 8,103
− 778
7,325

Down

A. 2,000
− 453
1,547   B. 8,081
− 778
7,303

C. 4,005
− 723
3,282   D. 7,019
− 284
6,735

Across

H. 9,300
− 659
8,641   L. 6,000
− 568
5,432   M. 3,018
− 716
2,302   N. 9,870
− 239
9,631

Down

H. 9,460
− 931
8,529   I. 7,032
− 596
6,436   J. 4,470
− 167
4,303   K. 1,506
− 285
1,221

74 4 digits minus 3 digits with regrouping across zeros

Cool Treats

Name _____ Date _____

Subtract.
Show your work.
Use your answers to complete each puzzle.

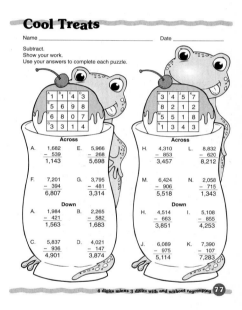

Across

A. 1,682
− 539
1,143   E. 5,966
− 268
5,698

F. 7,201
− 394
6,807   G. 3,795
− 481
3,314

Down

A. 1,984
− 421
1,563   B. 2,265
− 582
1,683

C. 5,837
− 936
4,901   D. 4,021
− 147
3,874

Across

H. 4,310
− 853
3,457   L. 8,832
− 620
8,212

M. 6,424
− 906
5,518   N. 2,058
− 715
1,343

Down

H. 4,514
− 663
3,851   I. 5,108
− 855
4,253

J. 6,089
− 975
5,114   K. 7,390
− 107
7,283

77 4 digits minus 3 digits with and without regrouping

Teamwork

Name _____ Date _____

Subtract.
Show your work.

COOKIES

1,930 − 539 **1,391**	5,040 − 442 **4,598**	9,470 − 315 **9,155**	6,027 − 762 **5,265**
2,006 − 658 **1,348**	6,908 − 746 **6,162**	9,000 − 853 **8,147**	5,050 − 989 **4,061**
3,200 − 561 **2,639**	7,051 − 479 **6,572**	8,093 − 338 **7,755**	4,510 − 693 **3,817**
4,720 − 686 **4,034**	8,006 − 795 **7,211**	7,008 − 821 **6,187**	3,000 − 914 **2,086**

72 4 digits minus 3 digits with regrouping across zeros

Candid Calculations

Name _____ Date _____

Subtract.
Show your work.

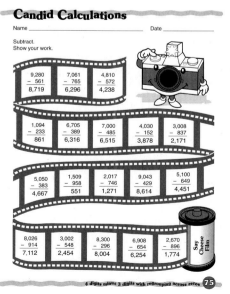

9,280 − 561 **8,719**	7,061 − 765 **6,296**	4,810 − 572 **4,238**
1,094 − 233 **861**	6,705 − 389 **6,316**	7,000 − 485 **6,515**	4,030 − 152 **3,878**	3,008 − 837 **2,171**
5,050 − 383 **4,667**	1,509 − 958 **551**	2,017 − 746 **1,271**	9,043 − 429 **8,614**	5,100 − 649 **4,451**
8,026 − 914 **7,112**	3,002 − 548 **2,454**	8,300 − 296 **8,004**	6,908 − 654 **6,254**	2,670 − 896 **1,774**

Say Cheese Film

75 4 digits minus 3 digits with regrouping across zeros

Just Buzzing Around!

Name _____ Date _____

Subtract.
Show your work.
Color the bee with the matching answer.

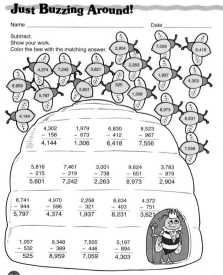

Bees: 2,904 · 7,059 · 6,418 · 4,374 · 7,242 · 3,621 · 2,263 · 1,937 · 4,303 · 8,959 · 5,797 · 5,601 · 525 · 1,306 · 4,144 · 8,973 · 8,231 · 7,556

4,302 − 158 **4,144**	1,979 − 673 **1,306**	6,830 − 412 **6,418**	8,523 − 967 **7,556**
5,816 − 215 **5,601**	7,461 − 219 **7,242**	3,001 − 738 **2,263**	9,624 − 651 **8,973**	3,783 − 879 **2,904**
6,741 − 944 **5,797**	4,970 − 596 **4,374**	2,258 − 321 **1,937**	8,634 − 403 **8,231**	4,372 − 751 **3,621**
1,057 − 532 **525**	9,348 − 389 **8,959**	7,505 − 446 **7,059**	5,197 − 894 **4,303**

78 4 digits minus 3 digits with and without regrouping

So Hard to Choose!

Subtract.
Show your work on another sheet of paper.
If the answer is correct, color the car.

New Car Lot

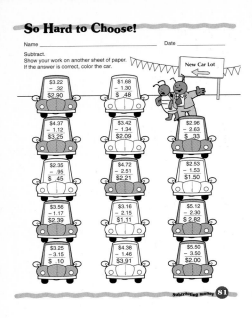

$3.22 − .32 = $2.90	$1.68 − 1.30 = $.48	$2.96 − 2.63 = $.33
$4.37 − 1.12 = $3.25	$3.42 − 1.34 = $2.09	$2.53 − 1.53 = $1.50
$2.35 − .95 = $.45	$4.72 − 2.51 = $2.21	$5.12 − 2.30 = $2.82
$3.56 − 1.17 = $2.39	$3.16 − 2.15 = $1.11	$5.50 − 3.50 = $2.00
$3.25 − 3.15 = $.10	$4.38 − 1.46 = $3.91	

Batter Up!

Read.
Solve.
Show your work.

A. Ben has $8.25. He pays $4.00 to watch the baseball game. How much money does Ben have left? **$4.25**

B. Tommy has $4.75. A hot dog costs $2.50. He buys one hot dog. How much money does Tommy have left? **$2.25**

C. Sarah has $6.00. She buys a bat for $3.50. How much money does Sarah have left? **$2.50**

D. Jamie has $12.75. He buys a baseball cap for $7.35. How much money does Jamie have left? **$5.40**

E. Abbey has $5.20. A box of popcorn costs $3.50. She buys a box. How much money does Abbey have left? **$1.70**

F. Scott has $16.00. He buys a T-shirt for $13.50. How much money does Scott have left? **$2.50**

Sunny Days

Estimate each difference by rounding to the nearest ten.
Color the petal with the matching answer.

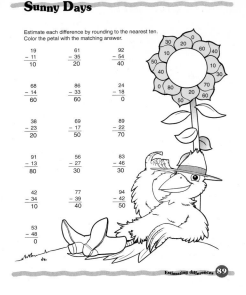

19 − 11 = 10	61 − 35 = 20	92 − 54 = 40
68 − 14 = 60	86 − 33 = 60	24 − 18 = 0
38 − 23 = 20	69 − 17 = 50	89 − 22 = 70
91 − 13 = 80	56 − 27 = 30	83 − 46 = 30
42 − 34 = 10	77 − 39 = 40	94 − 42 = 50
53 − 48 = 0		

Petal numbers: 30, 20, 60, 40, 10, 10, 30, 0, 80, 70, 50, 20, 50

Aha!

Subtract.
Show your work.
Color by the code.

Color Code
Between $.01 and $.99—blue
Between $1.00 and $1.99—brown
Between $2.00 and $2.99—red
Between $3.00 and $3.99—yellow

$7.50 − 5.20 = 2.30	$4.80 − 3.10 = 1.70	
$1.20 − .90 = .30	$3.80 − 2.70 = 1.10	
$4.25 − 3.35 = .90	$2.60 − 1.80 = .80	
$5.20 − 2.30 = 2.90	$3.75 − 3.60 = .15	
$8.00 − 4.50 = 3.50	$4.95 − 2.00 = 2.95	$7.06 − 4.04 = 3.02
$2.25 − .35 = 1.90	$4.10 − 2.50 = 1.60	
$5.50 − 1.70 = 3.80	$5.30 − 2.50 = 2.80	$5.10 − 1.11 = 3.99

Gone Fishing

Estimate each difference by rounding to the nearest ten.

62 − 18 → 60 − 20 = 40

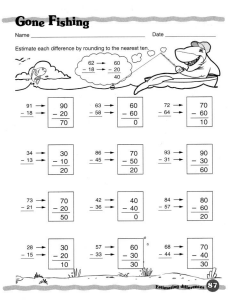

91 − 18 → 90 − 20 = 70	63 − 58 → 60 − 60 = 0	72 − 64 → 70 − 60 = 10
34 − 13 → 30 − 10 = 20	86 − 45 → 70 − 50 = 20	93 − 31 → 90 − 30 = 60
73 − 21 → 70 − 20 = 50	42 − 36 → 40 − 40 = 0	84 − 57 → 80 − 60 = 20
28 − 15 → 30 − 20 = 10	57 − 33 → 60 − 30 = 30	68 − 44 → 70 − 40 = 30

Downhill Divas

Estimate each difference by rounding to the nearest hundred.

470 − 210 → 500 − 200 = 300

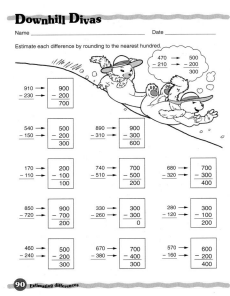

910 − 230 → 900 − 200 = 700		
540 − 150 → 500 − 200 = 300	890 − 310 → 900 − 300 = 600	
170 − 110 → 200 − 100 = 100	740 − 510 → 700 − 500 = 200	680 − 320 → 700 − 300 = 400
850 − 720 → 900 − 700 = 200	330 − 260 → 300 − 300 = 0	280 − 120 → 300 − 100 = 200
460 − 240 → 500 − 200 = 300	670 − 380 → 700 − 400 = 300	570 − 160 → 600 − 200 = 400

Drum Roll, Please!

Subtract.
Show your work.
Help Danny find his drummer.
Color each box with a difference that is less than $3.50.

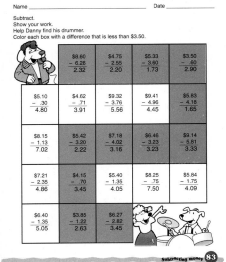

	$8.60 − 6.28 = 2.32	$4.75 − 2.55 = 2.20	$5.33 − 3.60 = 1.73	$3.50 − .60 = 2.90
$5.10 − .30 = 4.80	$4.62 − .71 = 3.91	$9.32 − 3.76 = 5.56	$9.41 − 4.96 = 4.45	$5.83 − 4.18 = 1.65
$8.15 − 1.13 = 7.02	$5.42 − 3.20 = 2.22	$7.18 − 4.02 = 3.16	$6.46 − 3.23 = 3.23	$9.14 − 5.81 = 3.33
$7.21 − 2.35 = 4.86	$4.15 − .70 = 3.45	$5.40 − 1.35 = 4.05	$8.25 − .75 = 7.50	$5.84 − 1.75 = 4.09
$6.40 − 1.35 = 5.05	$3.85 − 1.22 = 2.63	$6.27 − 2.82 = 3.45		

Cock-a-doodle-doo!

Estimate each difference by rounding to the nearest ten.

47 − 31 → 50 − 30 = 20

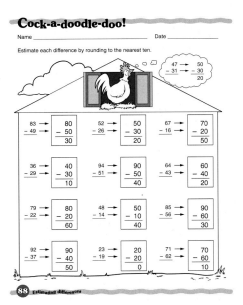

83 − 49 → 80 − 50 = 30	52 − 26 → 50 − 30 = 20	67 − 16 → 70 − 20 = 50
36 − 29 → 40 − 30 = 10	94 − 51 → 90 − 50 = 40	64 − 43 → 60 − 40 = 20
79 − 22 → 80 − 20 = 60	48 − 14 → 50 − 10 = 40	85 − 56 → 90 − 60 = 30
92 − 37 → 90 − 40 = 50	23 − 19 → 20 − 20 = 0	71 − 62 → 70 − 60 = 10

Time to Celebrate

Estimate each difference by rounding to the nearest hundred.

390 − 130 → 400 − 100 = 300

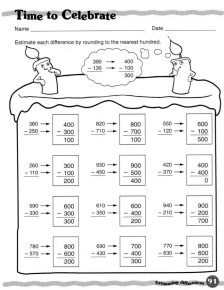

380 − 250 → 400 − 300 = 100	820 − 710 → 800 − 700 = 100	550 − 120 → 600 − 100 = 500
260 − 110 → 300 − 100 = 200	930 − 450 → 900 − 500 = 400	420 − 370 → 400 − 400 = 0
590 − 330 → 600 − 300 = 300	610 − 350 → 600 − 400 = 200	940 − 210 → 900 − 200 = 700
780 − 570 → 800 − 600 = 200	690 − 430 → 700 − 400 = 300	770 − 630 → 800 − 600 = 200

Coconuts in Paradise

Name _____ Date _____

Estimate each difference by rounding to the nearest hundred.
Cross off the matching answer on the palm tree.

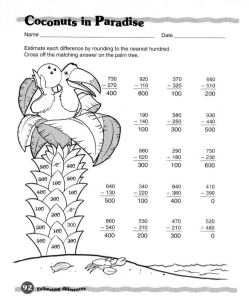

730 − 270 = 400	920 − 110 = 800	370 − 320 = 100	660 − 510 = 200
190 − 140 = 100	580 − 250 = 300	930 − 440 = 500	
880 − 620 = 300	290 − 180 = 100	750 − 230 = 600	
640 − 130 = 500	340 − 220 = 100	840 − 380 = 400	410 − 390 = 0
860 − 540 = 400	530 − 310 = 200	470 − 210 = 300	520 − 480 = 0

Palm tree answers: 500, 0, 400, 600, 100, 800, 400, 100, 300, 400, 100, 300, 100, 0, 8, 200, 300, 300, 500, 400

92 Estimating differences

How Does Your Garden Grow?

Name _____ Date _____

Read.
Solve.
Show your work.

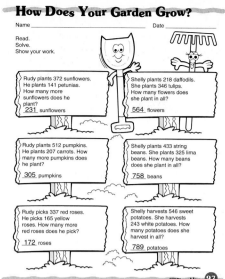

Rudy plants 372 sunflowers. He plants 141 petunias. How many more sunflowers does he plant?
231 sunflowers

Shelly plants 218 daffodils. She plants 346 tulips. How many flowers does she plant in all?
564 flowers

Rudy plants 512 pumpkins. He plants 207 carrots. How many more pumpkins does he plant?
305 pumpkins

Shelly plants 433 string beans. She plants 325 lima beans. How many beans does she plant in all?
758 beans

Rudy picks 337 red roses. He picks 165 yellow roses. How many more red roses does he pick?
172 roses

Shelly harvests 546 sweet potatoes. She harvests 243 white potatoes. How many potatoes does she harvest in all?
789 potatoes

Story problems 97

Page 105
Checkup 2
Test A
A. 79, 48, 17, 59, 28
B. 37, 3, 46, 19, 89
C. 65, 78, 89, 55, 16
D. 66, 37, 29, 75, 48
E. 54, 27, 68, 88, 8

Test B
A. 19, 9, 77, 37, 57
B. 87, 69, 44, 27, 67
C. 36, 16, 79, 68, 89
D. 48, 85, 28, 58, 35
E. 25, 59, 76, 48, 18

Proud Button Collectors

Name _____ Date _____

Read.
Solve.
Show your work.

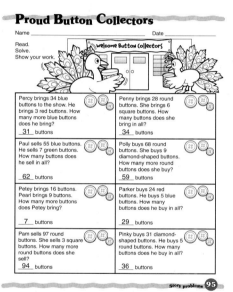

Percy brings 34 blue buttons to the show. He brings 3 red buttons. How many more blue buttons does he bring?
31 buttons

Penny brings 28 round buttons. She brings 6 square buttons. How many buttons does she bring in all?
34 buttons

Paul sells 55 blue buttons. He sells 7 green buttons. How many buttons does he sell in all?
62 buttons

Polly buys 68 round buttons. She buys 9 diamond-shaped buttons. How many more round buttons does she buy?
59 buttons

Petey brings 16 buttons. Pearl brings 9 buttons. How many more buttons does Petey bring?
7 buttons

Parker buys 24 red buttons. He buys 5 blue buttons. How many buttons does he buy in all?
29 buttons

Pam sells 97 round buttons. She sells 3 square buttons. How many more round buttons does she sell?
94 buttons

Pinky buys 31 diamond-shaped buttons. He buys 5 round buttons. How many buttons does he buy in all?
36 buttons

Story problems 95

Hit the Road!

Name _____ Date _____

Read.
Solve.
Show your work.

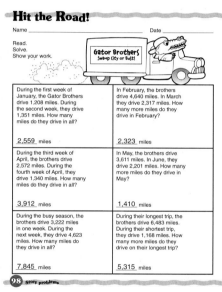

Gator Brothers
Swamp City or Bust!

During the first week of January, the Gator Brothers drive 1,208 miles. During the second week, they drive 1,351 miles. How many miles do they drive in all?
2,559 miles

In February, the brothers drive 4,640 miles. In March they drive 2,317 miles. How many more miles do they drive in February?
2,323 miles

During the third week of April, the brothers drive 2,572 miles. During the fourth week of April, they drive 1,340 miles. How many miles do they drive in all?
3,912 miles

In May, the brothers drive 3,611 miles. In June, they drive 2,201 miles. How many more miles do they drive in May?
1,410 miles

During the busy season, the brothers drive 3,222 miles in one week. During the next week, they drive 4,623 miles. How many miles do they drive in all?
7,845 miles

During their longest trip, the brothers drive 6,483 miles. During their shortest trip, they drive 1,168 miles. How many more miles do they drive on their longest trip?
5,315 miles

98 Story problems

Page 107
Checkup 3
Test A
A. 12, 27, 52, 14, 52
B. 34, 32, 14, 23, 31
C. 21, 15, 1, 21, 12
D. 31, 11, 55, 64, 33
E. 16, 32, 35, 2, 22

Test B
A. 12, 22, 14, 13, 21
B. 45, 1, 12, 42, 31
C. 21, 33, 61, 24, 50
D. 21, 17, 42, 13, 53
E. 33, 52, 22, 26, 42

A Day at the Doughnut Shop

Name _____ Date _____

Read.
Solve.
Show your work.

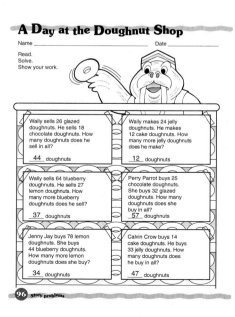

Wally sells 26 glazed doughnuts. He sells 18 chocolate doughnuts. How many doughnuts does he sell in all?
44 doughnuts

Wally makes 24 jelly doughnuts. He makes 12 cake doughnuts. How many more jelly doughnuts does he make?
12 doughnuts

Wally sells 64 blueberry doughnuts. He sells 27 lemon doughnuts. How many more blueberry doughnuts does he sell?
37 doughnuts

Perry Parrot buys 25 chocolate doughnuts. She buys 32 glazed doughnuts. How many doughnuts does she buy in all?
57 doughnuts

Jenny Jay buys 78 lemon doughnuts. She buys 44 blueberry doughnuts. How many more lemon doughnuts does she buy?
34 doughnuts

Calvin Crow buys 14 cake doughnuts. He buys 33 jelly doughnuts. How many doughnuts does he buy in all?
47 doughnuts

96 Story problems

Page 103
Checkup 1
Test A
A. 12, 83, 51, 31, 61
B. 58, 72, 32, 15, 43
C. 60, 22, 71, 43, 81
D. 91, 24, 62, 44, 22
E. 83, 52, 32, 61, 93

Test B
A. 41, 21, 52, 14, 62
B. 23, 64, 13, 31, 93
C. 52, 71, 33, 43, 83
D. 84, 34, 42, 21, 74
E. 13, 65, 92, 55, 81

Page 109
Checkup 4
Test A
A. 37, 39, 33, 29, 5
B. 29, 6, 35, 24, 19
C. 38, 18, 18, 26, 25
D. 19, 4, 47, 44, 27
E. 46, 58, 46, 8, 57

Test B
A. 9, 36, 26, 19, 39
B. 9, 22, 17, 47, 15
C. 17, 6, 26, 23, 78
D. 19, 67, 8, 29, 8
E. 25, 69, 25, 18, 58

Page 111
Checkup 5
Test A
A. 542, 953, 623, 216, 171
B. 702, 652, 337, 431, 248
C. 431, 746, 112, 945, 434
D. 552, 226, 332, 812, 925
E. 650, 361, 551, 214, 834

Test B
A. 310, 184, 961, 610, 856
B. 470, 322, 824, 157, 522
C. 111, 761, 921, 611, 407
D. 455, 614, 243, 833, 523
E. 544, 743, 136, 332, 712

Page 113
Checkup 6
Test A
A. 409, 688, 328, 39, 443
B. 891, 362, 52, 549, 177
C. 246, 487, 825, 572, 67
D. 398, 175, 307, 806, 853
E. 559, 746, 854, 471, 248

Test B
A. 26, 518, 816, 438, 934
B. 247, 766, 585, 289, 646
C. 177, 657, 555, 862, 439
D. 877, 591, 225, 672, 448
E. 353, 579, 354, 86, 769

Page 115
Checkup 7
Test A
A. 394, 262, 218, 259, 549
B. 186, 365, 59, 26, 385
C. 179, 129, 434, 91, 268
D. 164, 145, 77, 39, 307
E. 183, 681, 309, 89, 552

Test B
A. 325, 179, 377, 151, 548
B. 219, 475, 86, 267, 108
C. 223, 278, 159, 539, 239
D. 49, 391, 442, 83, 387
E. 155, 107, 408, 378, 274

Page 117
Checkup 8
Test A
A. 88, 364, 275, 174, 31
B. 589, 337, 286, 24, 48
C. 418, 171, 106, 177, 513
D. 58, 227, 56, 776, 356
E. 78, 243, 235, 129, 113

Test B
A. 65, 217, 354, 413, 347
B. 44, 27, 637, 33, 72
C. 35, 519, 129, 655, 478
D. 434, 35, 139, 186, 76
E. 169, 218, 153, 36, 436

Page 119
Checkup 9
Test A
A. 3,766; 3,155; 8,391; 4,674; 8,525
B. 9,406; 3,806; 2,336; 8,067; 5,775
C. 3,275; 6,769; 4,178; 929; 1,388
D. 2,521; 5,891; 8,626; 3,662; 7,788
E. 4,690; 2,653; 2,573; 6,421; 5,578

Test B
A. 8,463; 5,624; 2,756; 5,716; 1,781
B. 2,887; 6,238; 3,274; 5,383; 8,057
C. 2,186; 3,469; 7,617; 670; 4,846
D. 6,494; 2,289; 8,774; 4,268; 5,939
E. 7,576; 6,903; 2,390; 9,086; 645

Page 121
Checkup 10
Test A
A. 6,427; 5,322; 8,088; 7,716; 3,877
B. 8,685; 7,314; 2,061; 6,022; 5,808
C. 7,334; 8,083; 7,511; 6,386; 3,176
D. 6,108; 4,315; 7,335; 2,431; 8,581
E. 5,484; 7,639; 7,241; 4,176; 8,214

Test B
A. 5,387; 4,448; 7,622; 1,441; 8,818
B. 3,719; 8,452; 4,741; 7,627; 6,007
C. 8,446; 3,028; 7,533; 6,738; 5,741
D. 2,858; 7,652; 7,183; 4,322; 8,607
E. 7,323; 7,004; 2,537; 8,855; 5,227